ONE
MINUTE
ALONE
WITH
GOD
FOR
MEN

BOB BARNES

HARVEST HOUSE PUBLISHERS
EUGENE, OREGON

Cover by Dugan Design Group, Bloomington, Minnesota

Cover photo © Dugan Design Group

ONE MINUTE ALONE WITH GOD FOR MEN
Copyright © 2013 by Bob Barnes
Published by Harvest House Publishers
Eugene, Oregon 97402
www.harvesthousepublishers.com

ISBN 978-0-7369-5081-7
ISBN 978-0-7369-5082-4 (eBook)

Printed in China

13 14 15 16 17 18 19 20 21 / RDS-GLD / 10 9 8 7 6 5 4 3 2 1

To: _____

From: _____

Date: _____

Dedication

This book is dedicated to my loving parents, J.K. and Gertie Barnes. They gave me the early training to believe and trust in the Lord Jesus. They were farm people in their early years, so we didn't have many material provisions, but they were rich in family love. As three boys, Billy, Kenneth, and I never knew we weren't rich because Mom and Dad made us worthy.

Though they have been long gone to heaven, they are still alive in who I am. Thank you both.

Why One Minute
Makes a Difference

We are so busy trying to keep up the hectic pace required to get things done that we often miss out on receiving the strength and leading we need from God in order to live our lives. Our short attention spans make us restless, and we want to move on to the next subject or the next show or the next activity. This is so common that many of us don't stay focused on God for more than a fleeting "help me" prayer.

If I told you that you had to commit to fifteen minutes a day, you might not want to give that much time to God. However, who doesn't have one minute? God sacrificed His Son on the cross for us; certainly we can sacrifice one minute of our time and attention. My desire is that you'll be so caught up in the versatility of the topics that you can't put the book down. You can skip around to various topics or read it in order. Either way, if you make this a regular commitment for at least 21 consecutive days, you will be forming a new healthy-faith habit. Hopefully a habit that will last a lifetime.

Men often ask me, "How do I live out my Christian faith?" The answer is found when you seek stories, wisdom, and insight from men who have experienced the ups and downs of the Christian walk. I've attempted to make this book very practical by using stories out of my life experiences or those that men can identify with. Enjoy your journey as you grow in learning how to live out the Christian faith.

Bob

Contents

One Minute
Alone with God
Prayer

Father God, I am on the journey of life with You. It is an adventure, a challenge, and a privilege to become the man You have created me to be. I'm thankful to have You in my life. As I walk this devotional path in the next days and weeks, I long to get to know You and to be known by You completely. What do You see in my heart, Lord? Where do You want me to go from here? In what ways do You want me to encourage my family and friends in their walks with You?

I want to grow in Your strengths and purposes. I've had seasons of feeling stuck. But I'm eager and ready to invest my heart and soul in discovering how to be a man of God. Amen.

Have You Left Your First Love?

*I hold this against you: You have
forsaken the love you had at first.*

REVELATION 2:4

Can you remember the excitement you felt when you first responded to the call of Jesus? I know I can. I was 12 years old, and it was on Easter Sunday. Our wonderful Sunday school teacher finished each lesson encouraging us to accept Jesus as our personal Savior. On that special Sunday, I responded to the pastor's invitation to become saved. That decision made it possible for me to make all my other decisions in life.

Many times I ask myself, "Why do I do what I do?" I realize that sometimes I'm doing good things but for the wrong reasons. Jesus taught that we aren't to do good to gain heaven. Our love for Jesus should motivate our works.

Paul told the church in Ephesus that he'd heard of their love of their faith and the love for all the saints (Ephesians 1:15-16). However, 30 years later, John, the writer of Revelation, was reproving the church for abandoning their first love. They were doing a lot of good things, but not out of love for Him. Do a reality check and see why you do what you do. And then let that powerful love you first had for God guide your days.

Father God, may my actions reflect my first love for You. Guide me in eliminating any wrong motives for doing good works. I truly want to be motivated by faith in You. Amen.

Lasting Joy

He put a new song in my mouth,
a hymn of praise to our God.

PSALM 40:3

Now that our children are grown and our grandchildren are almost grown, Emilie and I have time to reminisce about the first days of school, graduation ceremonies, sporting events, birthday parties, holidays, and weddings. What a gift of delight these memories are.

What would life be like without the joy? Even with all the happy occasions you have experienced, God is the one source of lasting joy. When we come before God with an open heart and words of confession, He is just and will forgive us of all unrighteousness (1 John 1:9). In the emptying of our old self, God gives us hymns of praise and a new song, one written just for you. This is eternal joy, my friend.

When the children are gone, or when you are spending longer stretches at home on your own, what will you hear? I hope it's the echo of past laughter, the ringing in of new celebrations, and the joy of eternal salvation through your sweet Lord.

Lord, let me take time to savor the daily joys with my family. And give me gratitude for Your gift of eternal life. This is my source of joy forever. Amen.

Love Without Measure

Love is patient, love is kind. It does not envy,
it does not boast, it is not proud.

1 CORINTHIANS 13:4

To love as Christ loved is to love without measure. Paul, the apostle, describes the Christian view of love for the Corinthians. Look at the attributes listed in 1 Corinthians 13:4-8:

- Love is patient.
- Love is kind.
- Love is not jealous.
- Love doesn't brag.
- Love is not arrogant.
- Love does not seek its own.
- Love is not provoked.
- Love does not get even.
- Love does not rejoice in sin.
- Love rejoices with truth.
- Love bears all things.
- Love believes all things.
- Love endures all things.
- Love never fails.

This life-changing love will impact all that you say, do, and believe. Love your wife, family, friends, and strangers with this love without measure.

God, let me love without measure. We live in a world that wants to put a quantitative scale on love. I want to love as You love. Amen.

A Father's Open Arms

I tell you, there is rejoicing in the presence of the
angels of God over one sinner who repents.

Luke 15:10

One of the great stories in the New Testament is that of the prodigal son, found in Luke 15:11-32. I encourage you to read this story of a father's great love. The younger son asked his father for an early inheritance so he could leave home and live a life of pleasure without restriction or responsibility. And the result? He lost all of his money and ended up wallowing with the pigs. In the pit of despair, the son realized he was living a sinful life.

The son returned home telling his father that he was no longer worthy to be his son. So imagine his shock and joy when his dad ran to embrace and kiss him with great compassion and forgiveness.

Do you relate to the father or to the son? Maybe you relate to the older son and have remained dutiful to your family or your job while watching another person mess up and then receive forgiveness. No matter who you relate to in this story, we should embrace its message of love's capacity to overcome human failings.

Lord, help me become a man who seeks Your unconditional love. Protect me from pride or jealousy so that I come to You with my every weakness and am quick to forgive others. Amen.

Your Sins Will Find You Out

Nothing in all creation is hidden from God's sight.
Everything is uncovered and laid bare before the eyes
of him to whom we must give account.

HEBREWS 4:13

In my morning newspaper, I read that another well-known personality has fallen. Like so many fallen icons before him, he thought he could hide his behavior from his inner circle.

My mother used to tell us boys, "Be careful—your sins will find you out." I'm sure that this man's mother told him the same thing. Even if we are able to hide our sin from the people around us for a while, nothing is ever hidden from God's sight. God sees everything we do and think.

If we find ourselves in an act, a thought, or a lifestyle that we need to confess, I have relied on a great verse that helps me "rebound" from a secret that I am trying to hide from God and others: "If we confess our sins, he is faithful and just and will forgive us our sins and purify us from all unrighteousness" (1 John 1:9).

Don't let unconfessed, so-called hidden sins come between you and God.

Father God, I thank You for this revelation that I can escape my secret sins—You are here to give me a way out of darkness and back into the light. Amen.

Have a Pure Heart

*Finally then, brethren, we urge and exhort in
the Lord Jesus that you should abound more and
more, just as you received from us how you ought
to walk and to please God; for you know what
commandments we gave you through the Lord Jesus.*

1 Thessalonians 4:1-2 nkjv

Purity is becoming rather obsolete in our culture. There was a time when we were challenged as young people and adults to live a life of purity. We could look up to athletes, pastors, and politicians as our role models because many of them embraced a life of purity and integrity. That seems to be less true all the time.

Even those of us who claim to be followers of Jesus often sidestep every scripture that teaches us to seek purity. But a pure heart is the byproduct of living out in real life what Scripture tells us. It's time for us to be a positive witness for whom and for what we stand.

Humble yourself to recognize the righteousness of God. Be willing to have a pure heart.

Father, I want a heart that knows and loves You. One that is pure in spirit. I want to be a doer of Your Word. Amen.

What Is in Your Heart?

You are already clean because of the
word I have spoken to you.

JOHN 15:3

After one of my wife Emilie's speaking engagements, a lady stood in line to have Emilie autograph a copy of her book. As the woman watched Emilie sign the page, she said, "I like your books because they are clean." Emilie replied, "Thank you. It's not hard for me to write clean stories because that's the way I think."

The computer era has a saying: "Junk in junk out!" You are what you think and take in. Our speech and actions flow from the inside out. Is your heart clean? I recently read a quote from John Wesley from around 1730 on this subject, and he states that believers are "purified from pride by the deepest poverty of spirit; from anger, from every unkind or turbulent passion, by meekness and gentleness; from every desire but to please and enjoy God, to know and love him more and more." Examine what is going into your heart and mind each day. Immerse yourself in God's promises and commands. Experience the power of a heart that seeks to know and love God more each day.

God, thank You for Your grace and redemption. Give me a hunger to be filled with Your truth and mercy. Let all that flows from my heart be pleasing to You. Amen.

Honoring Fatherhood

Grandchildren are the crown of old men,
and the glory of sons is their fathers.

PROVERBS 17:6 NASB

Fathers play a vital role in developing a child's awareness of God's authority. Children learn what it means to honor God by watching their father's words and actions. As we long to be good fathers, we should also pray that children honor fatherhood through...

- love,
- submission,
- godliness,
- admiration, and
- respect for his leadership.

Children are blessed by honoring their fathers. But obedience isn't always easy. Many of us probably struggled to respect our parents a time or two, right? But at least we grew up with a bit more reinforcement from our culture to respect others. These days, we see an assortment of father figures on television who fumble around, can't make a decision to save their lives, and watch with bewilderment as their kids run the house. It's time to reclaim fatherhood as a position of honor and value. You and I, we need to make a deliberate effort each day to be the men God called us to be. Give your children a reason to honor you, the role of fatherhood, and the authority of God in their lives.

Father God, instill in me a strength to express Your authority and wisdom so that my children respect me and come to know the might of a right relationship with You. Amen.

Becoming a Father to Honor

Honor your father and mother.

EXODUS 20:12

What is a father? In the midst of many demands and worries, it can be easy to forget what a father is or what a father can be. Whether you are a father, uncle, brother, or husband, let this acrostic inspire you to strive to be honorable in every way:

F – Faithful in following Jesus
A – Allows God to make him all he can be
T – Thanks God for all His blessings
H – Holy in his approach to life
E – Expresses love to those around him
R – Responds to God's teachings in Scripture

Are these a part of your path? Which ones are the most difficult for you to measure up to? Spend time reading the Bible, talking to other fathers of faith, and praying for guidance. Memorize this list or jot it down and keep it in your car or at the office as a reminder of the harvest of godly traits that are yours when you walk in the way of God.

Father God, give me the desire to be the father You would like for me to be. I need Your strength and encouragement each day. Surround me with other men who have the same desire. Amen.

Building on the Cornerstone

Jesus is "'the stone you builders rejected,
which has become the cornerstone.'
Salvation is found in no one else, for there
is no other name under heaven given to
mankind by which we must be saved."

ACTS 4:11-12

I have a good friend who is a respected bricklayer and masonry contractor. He learned his trade from his father, who came to America as a young man from Italy. He tells me the first thing he does when he gets on the job is gather data and measurements so he can pinpoint where the cornerstone should be. Everything will be built from this central calculation. All heights of retaining walls will come from there. The security and longevity of the structure depends on the strength of the cornerstone.

The verse for today reveals that Jesus is our cornerstone. The life you're living will have that kind of strength and lasting value when you make Christ your cornerstone for every decision, belief, and hope. When another aspect of your character is being formed, make sure that it measures up to God's standard. Build a life that stands firmly on the foundation of Jesus.

God, You have provided me with a cornerstone that cannot be moved, broken, or destroyed. Show me how to build a life of great significance and strength on the foundation of Christ. Amen.

One Minute
Alone with God
Prayer

Father God, when I wake up in the morning, my first thoughts are often of the schedule, tasks, or needs ahead. I want to start my day by thinking of You, my source for hope, strength, and life. Give me a grateful heart that is eager to praise You for the opportunity of a new beginning. Where I have fear, give me peace. If I am concerned about how to provide for myself and my family, restore my belief in Your care for our every need. And when I find it difficult to get out of bed and face another day, remind me that it is a gift from You. Give me the courage to accept this day and to offer it back to You so that You can shape it in mighty ways. Amen.

Godly Money Guidelines

*The earth is the LORD's and all it contains,
the world, and those who dwell in it.*

PSALM 24:1 NASB

Many people only think about God in relation to their money when they're contributing to the offering plate on Sunday. But we need God's guidance and wisdom for all of our money matters. Here are some guidelines to help you give your earthly wealth God's care:

1. Recognize that God owns everything. God holds us responsible to faithfully manage for Him any money or possessions He gives us.

2. Know that the goal of financial responsibility is financial freedom. You can achieve this by paying your debts, not spending more than you make, giving to God and His children, and being thankful for what you have.

3. Establish that your spiritual purpose is to serve God. When you do this, all of your resources work toward that end. Always ask yourself if a purchase feeds or detracts from your spiritual purpose.

4. Give money to the Lord regularly. God doesn't need our money to fulfill His purpose, but He will use what we obediently and willingly give to minister to others, and we will receive a blessing in return.

Father God, You know that this is an area I struggle with. Give me the desire and courage to take leadership in this part of my life. Amen.

Cultivating Intimacy

*Be kind and compassionate to one another, forgiving
each other, just as in Christ God forgave you.*

EPHESIANS 4:32

Whatever happened to intimacy? Sex is everywhere, but intimacy is rare. Even our basic communication has shifted from intimate to public. Emails and social networking are about connecting to *more* people instead of connecting *more* with a person who matters to us.

Here are some steps you can take to restore the warmth of sincere intimacy with your wife:

Step One: Demonstrate tenderness and warmth. Hold hands. Cuddle. Place your arm on her shoulders when you are walking together.

Step Two: Be liberal with praise. Express gratitude for how she cares for you and the family, serves God and others, and is a person you admire.

Step Three: Take breaks for conversation. Put down the paper, stop watching television, or put aside your work and make time for casual dialogue. Make eye contact and be present.

Step Four: Share your heart. Intimacy is created when you are willing to be transparent and open with your wife and children.

Father God, may I be able to create intimacy with my wife each day. Let me desire to know her and to be known by her. Amen.

Protect Your Mind and Heart

Above all else, guard your heart, for
everything you do flows from it.

Proverbs 4:23

We are the product of the decisions we make each day of our life. That's why Proverbs tells us to watch over our hearts. We must protect ourselves from deceit, lust, pride, and many other potential pitfalls. A man fights the good fight in his mind all the time. This is where the enemy attacks our weak areas. Here are some ways for you to protect your heart, and in turn, keep your mind fixed on God's righteousness:

1. Know the truth. God's truth is the light to which you can hold up all questions, doubts, and concerns. Darkness fades and discernment illuminates the way.

2. Be aligned with God's Word. If what you think, hear, believe, or feel doesn't line up with what God tells you in Scripture, it needs to be rejected. As Jesus told Satan when He was being tempted, "Get behind me, Satan." You won't believe it or let it influence who you are. Using this as a criteria for what you read or see—you would reject most of what comes to your mind.

3. Share your discernment of truth with others. Lead others so that they won't be blindsided with false claims and statements. When you walk in godly wisdom, you will model the way for others.

God, You are the Alpha and the Omega (the beginning and the end). Let my soul be in line with Your truth and wisdom for every need I face and every decision I make. Amen.

Stand Tall in Your Walk

*Don't let anyone look down on you because you are
young, but set an example for the believers in speech, in
conduct, in love, in faith and in purity.*

1 TIMOTHY 4:12

Not just the young should follow Paul's instruction to
Timothy in our verse for today. We all must honor and serve
God in these areas:

Speech—Control what you say. Concentrate on the positive and stay away from the negative. Build up others.

Conduct—Practice good behavior. Look people in the
eye, give a strong, positive handshake, and exhibit good manners. Get caught doing something good.

Love—We are to love God and those around us. Others can discover God's love when they experience a human
expression of His grace.

Faith—Do you act to please man or God? People who put
their faith into action change lives.

Purity—Maintain integrity and honor in your life by
abstaining from gossip, sexual impurities, negative thoughts,
and deceptive behavior.

As James says, "Prove yourselves doers of the word, and
not merely hearers who delude themselves" (James 1:22
NASB). Our behavior is a great testimony of who God is and
our love for Him.

*Lord, let me examine each of these areas in my life this week.
Show me my weakness in each area. Give me the desire to help me
make necessary changes in each. Amen.*

Be Strong in Grace

My son, be strong in the grace
that is in Christ Jesus.

2 Timothy 2:1

In each of the letters Paul wrote to the various churches, he included three words: grace, mercy, and peace. I have always thought of these words in a mathematical formula: Grace + Mercy = Peace. When we understand grace and mercy, we'll have peace in our lives. These would be my three simple definitions of these words:

Grace—the unearned favor that saves us from sin
Mercy—the undeserved favor that forgives us because of
       our separation from God
Peace—the unsought favor that reconciles us to God

In Romans 11:5, Paul writes, "If by grace, then it cannot be based on works; if it were, grace would no longer be grace." And again, in Ephesians, he writes, "It is by grace you have been saved, through faith—and this is not from yourselves, it is the gift of God" (Ephesians 2:8).

All three of these words—grace, mercy, and peace—offer us the blessings we have within ourselves when we put our hope into the truth of God's Word.

Lord, may I awaken each day full of gratitude for my sal-
vation through Christ. It is only through Your grace, mercy, and
peace that I can receive this beautiful gift of eternity. Amen.

Knowing the Voice of the Lord

This is what the Sovereign LORD...says:
In repentance and rest is your salvation,
in quietness and trust is your strength.

ISAIAH 30:15

When we know the voice of God in the stillness, then we'll recognize His voice when we run into chaos or confusion. An American Indian was visiting the city of New York. As he strolled along the busy street of Park Avenue, he paused and told his host to be quiet because he heard a cricket. The host asked him how he could hear a cricket with all the noise in the city. The Indian replied that it was because he had learned to hear the cricket in the silence of the desert.

Take time to go for long walks or hikes. Spend time sitting on a park bench and watching the river flow by. Find ways to incorporate the spiritual discipline of being silent before the Lord. You will be amazed how clearly you will hear and know the voice of the Lord in the midst of life's busyness.

Father God, my quiet time alone with You is special—I consider it to be very sacred. Thanks for listening. Amen.

The Struggle of Being Tough and Tender

We were gentle among you,
just as a nursing mother
cherishes her own children.

1 THESSALONIANS 2:7 NKJV

The American way is to teach our boys to develop into men who are tough—we're not to cry when we get hurt. But some of the biggest men are the softest inside. John Wayne once lived down the street from us. He played tough guys in the movies but was a gentle man in real life.

The apostle Paul endured imprisonment, floggings, stonings, and shipwrecks (see 2 Corinthians 11:23-27). Obviously, he was tough. But today's verse reveals his tender side. He describes himself as being as gentle and tender as a loving mother is with her children.

I saw such an example of a tough and tender man when Barbara Walters interviewed the real-life Desert Storm hero "Stormin' Norman" Schwarzkopf. This tough military man had tears in his eyes as he talked about the Gulf War. Mrs. Walters asked, "Why, General, aren't you afraid to cry?" He replied without hesitation, "No, Mrs. Walters. I am afraid of a man who won't cry."

It takes strength to be tender for the Lord and your family. Showing both toughness and tenderness is becoming a whole man of God.

Father God, I want to break the male barrier of toughness to be able to show my tender side. Thanks for the encouragement. Amen.

Team Player

May the God who gives
endurance and encouragement
give you the same attitude of mind toward
each other that Christ Jesus had.

ROMANS 15:5

I vividly remember the encouragement that my high school and college basketball coaches would give me when they called me to the sidelines. As the coach explained the next play or strategy, he would put his arm on my shoulder. That simple touch said, "Bob, I believe in you. You can make it happen."

Athletics can truly encourage boys as they travel the path to manhood. It's an arena where we can see the tender sides of tough athletes, expressed when grown men jump into the arms of a teammate, two or more buddies high-five it, or a swarm of players jump on top of the player who made the big play. The childlike excitement is the tender side of the tough, not-to-be-beaten athlete.

Are you able to give your male friends a pat on the back? We all need some encouragement as we head onto the field to make the big plays in life. We need each other if we're going to be victorious in this game called life.

Lord, help me be an encourager to other men. I want to show Your attitude to people around me so that they are inspired and built up as members of Your team. Amen.

BC (Before Christ)

*Since, then, you have been raised with Christ, set your
hearts on things above, where Christ is, seated at the
right hand of God. Set your minds on things above,
not on earthly things... When Christ, who is your life,
appears, then you also will appear with him in glory.*

Colossians 3:1-3

In the third chapter of Colossians, Paul is encouraging
Christians to live out their new nature as believers.

Let's take a look at Colossians 3:5-9, which describes the
nature of man before Christ:

sexual immorality	impurity
lust	evil desires
greed	idolatry

These are the BC natures, which we are to shed because
we have the strength and righteousness as Christ through our
salvation. Continual renewing is necessary in order that the
new life may be strong in faith; so we can hold back the pre-
vious powers of nature.

Evaluate your life. Are you BC or AC? If you are still a
man who exhibits the nature of old, what are you going to
do about it?

*God, I want to shed the characteristics of my BC self. Help
me set my heart and mind on the things above. I want my focus
to be on You in all that I do. Show me the way to become a real
AC man. Amen.*

AC (After Christ)

*Put on the new self, which is being
renewed in knowledge
in the image of its Creator.*

Colossians 3:10

I had the pleasure of talking to a missionary couple about their prison ministry in Oregon. The husband meets with the men and the wife works with women prisoners and mentors the children of the inmates. They shared countless stories of how the Spirit of God changed prisoners' lives.

The BC and AC stories are only possible when God gets ahold of their hearts and breaks through their human nature. Through a Bible study and compassionate leaders, they realize how much they need God and His salvation. In their "After Christ" life, they, like all of us, receive the nature of the spiritual being described in Colossians 3:12-17:

compassion	kindness
humility	gentleness
patience	forgiveness

Continue to grow in these AC behaviors. Which ones are the hardest for you to embrace? Explore Scripture and discover all that you can about these traits. These are your new nature as a believer. Learn about them, live them, and share them as a man of God.

Father God, one of the great things about Scripture; it reveals the spirit of mankind. It exposes the bad and gives direction for the good. Give me a continual desire to know the truth. Amen.

One Minute
Alone with God
Prayer

Lord, You have shown me how it is possible to be strong and weak at once. When I give my weaknesses and needs to You, it is Your strength and power that works through me. During the times when I've tried to "go it alone" or succeed on the world's terms, I've always known that anything I built could crumble in the blink of an eye. But building a life in Your strength and upon the rock of Your presence, I feel the security I've always longed for. Don't let me be tempted to trade the solid truths and promises of Your will for a second-rate, man-made version of life. Amen.

Stay Flexible

Have mercy on me, my God, have
mercy on me, for in you I take refuge.
I will take refuge in the shadow of
your wings until the disaster has passed.

PSALM 57:1

In my early days, when I ran a plant that manufactured factory-built houses, business was slow, and we took on a most unique project. Our company was employed to build three portable laundry room units. We had never undertaken such a project. But in order to stay in business, we had to be flexible. It's a good thing we did—those three units saved our company.

Our flexibility as a company let us go on in our business endeavor. I learned a lot from that experience: I needed to firmly trust in God and understand that He was the overseer of the project.

Today's scripture expressed my situation when David prayed to God, "Have mercy on me, my God, have mercy on me, for in you I take refuge." You might feel stuck. But stand in God's refuge and be flexible. And never be discouraged by God's delay—continue in your trust in Him.

Father, You always amaze me. When I'm ready to give up You come alongside and give me support. Give me the wisdom and patience to be flexible and open to Your plan. Amen.

Be a Hero

Blessed are the poor in spirit, for theirs
is the kingdom of heaven.

MATTHEW 5:3

When I was young, my two brothers and I loved listening to *The Lone Ranger* radio show every Saturday night. I learned a lot of good life principles from that program. What was the masked man's secret for success? The Lone Ranger believed in these things:

- Tolerance—The Lone Ranger demonstrated acceptance of other races through his close relationship with the Native American friend, Tonto.
- Fairness—Each week, this hero supported the American tenet for each person's right to choose a lifework and to earn their way through individual effort.
- Patriotism—He showed his love of country by aiding churches, serving communities, and preserving law and honor.
- Sympathy—He chose the side of the oppressed in their time of need, demonstrating that a strong man can be compassionate.
- Religion—He modeled allowing people to worship God in their own ways. His confidantes were Native American Tonto and the Catholic padre.

Are you shedding light on the difference between good and evil through your actions? Even though we don't use silver bullets, we can use silver words to be a hero to another.

Father God, may I be able to pass on my values to the next generation, and may they be open to my wisdom. Amen.

A Marriage Made in Heaven

*That is why a man leaves his father and mother
and is united to his wife, and
they become one flesh.*

GENESIS 2:24

It was with great anticipation that I stood at the altar to perform the wedding ceremony for my granddaughter, Christine Merrihew, and her future husband, Patrick Ianni. In the months of preparation to join these two people together in a Christian ceremony, I thought back to Genesis. I realized this is the first recorded marriage in the Bible, and it has a lot to teach us today, when our nation is divided over what marriage is. A marriage vow is more than a contract that we can break. God created this covenant so that a man and a woman could become one for life.

As I stood with Christine and Patrick, we concluded the ceremony with prayer and the great announcement: "It gives me great honor to introduce to you for the first time Mr. and Mrs. Patrick Ianni." This proclamation was met with a loud applause. A union made in heaven deserves to be applauded.

Celebrate your own marriage by honoring your wife, your relationship, and the sacredness of this covenant between man and woman.

Father God, may our society realize the importance of marriage. Protect us from losing the original reason for marriage. Amen.

Labor for God

Not by way of eye service, as men-pleasers,
but as slaves of Christ, doing the will
of God from the heart.

EPHESIANS 6:6

In college, I studied the great civilizations and their perception of why people worked: It was to do work unto the Lord. Artists, builders, musicians, and theologians all seemed to create great pieces that reflected their Creator. In Europe, one can see the great cathedrals built to honor God, hear inspiring symphonies composed to praise the Lord, and watch plays written to reflect the glory of God.

Today, too many men experience burnout because they've made work their god instead of making their work an offering to God. As a Christian, you should bring your skill, passion, and faith to all that you do. Make your motivation about bringing honor to God rather than climbing a corporate ladder. You might just be amazed at how others grow to respect your redirected focus.

It's never too late. You can always turn the vessel around and head in the right way. Surrender your work to the Lord and watch what He can do through your offering!

Father, may the work of my hands and mind be a blessing to You. I give to You my job and efforts as ongoing sacrifices. Today, I exchange my goals for Your purpose. Amen.

Faithful Steward

Many rich people threw in large amounts. But a poor widow came and put in two very small copper coins, worth only a few cents. Calling his disciples to him, Jesus said, "Truly I tell you, this poor widow has put more into the treasury than all the others. They all gave out of their wealth; but she, out of her poverty, put in everything—all she had to live on."

MARK 12:41-44

In this verse, God celebrates the poor widow's offering, not because she gave a lot but because she faithfully gave what she had. God owns everything, but He has placed us in positions to be good managers of His possessions. When we do right, we are blessed. "The LORD your God will bless you in all your harvest and in all the work of your hands, and your joy will be complete" (Deuteronomy 16:15).

Throughout Scripture we're encouraged to be cheerful givers and stewards who sacrifice. My dad used to tell us boys, "It's not how much you make, but what you do with what you make." Make your money and your life count and follow the faithful example of the widow.

Lord, guide me to give of my money, time, self, and talents so that I serve You with a heart that is faithful. May my offering always be pleasing to You. Amen.

Where Is Your Treasure?

Store up for yourselves treasures in heaven,
where moths and vermin do not destroy,
and where thieves do not break in and steal.

MATTHEW 6:20-21

Our economy has been at a very serious low in recent years. The unemployment rate is soaring, welfare costs are increasing, and home foreclosures are increasing each month. When such a crisis happens, it actually helps us define and redefine our attitudes toward money. As we all look at our spending and saving habits, we have the opportunity to do things in a right and godly way. Review these questions and consider whether your answers line up with Scripture.

- How do I look at money?
- Should I avoid it?
- What do I do with it?
- What do I think about possessions? Am I a saver or spender?
- Am I more holy if I live without a lot of money?

A proper attitude toward money, property, and investments will reflect how we want to honor God with all our stuff. Someone once told me that he could look at my checkbook register to tell me how much I honor God. What does your checkbook say about your heart?

Father, all that I have is from You. Give me a heart for Your priorities. Amen.

Rules Give Freedom

This is love for God: to keep his commandments.
And his commands are not burdensome.

1 JOHN 5:3

Our culture strays from the principles of the Ten Commandments and is facing the consequences. It's time to review Exodus 20:1-17. Read through the whole passage, but here are the Ten Commandments in condensed format:

1. You shall have no other gods before me.
2. You shall not make for yourself an image in the form of anything...
3. You shall not misuse the name of the LORD your God.
4. Remember the Sabbath day by keeping it holy.
5. Honor your father and your mother.
6. You shall not murder.
7. You shall not commit adultery.
8. You shall not steal.
9. You shall not give false testimony against your neighbor.
10. You shall not covet...anything that belongs to your neighbor.

God's grace is all you truly need. But heeding the Ten Commandments gives you the freedom of obedience and faithfulness.

Father God, my freedom in Christ is beyond the law, but I would be wise to pay attention to the freedom Your rules provide for daily living. Give me a heart of obedience. Amen.

Why Read the Old Testament?

My word…goes out from my mouth:
it will not return to me empty.

ISAIAH 55:11

Our pastor recently shared that a new believer asked, "Do I have to read the Old Testament?" How many of us have asked the same question? The answer is "yes!"

The Old Testament sets the stage for the Advent of Jesus. This set of 39 books offers background essential to understanding the New Testament. When we study God's Word and put it to memory, it will be remembered and applied at the very time we need it. If we skip the Old Testament, we are missing out on vital instruction, covenants, and promises that are important to our lives as believers.

If the Old Testament seems boring or difficult, consider those pages an important journey you are to take in order to get a broad understanding of what God has done in history, what He's doing now, and what He plans to do in the future. Nothing is boring about that!

Father God, open my eyes as I journey into the unknown of the Old Testament. Help me draw inspiration and a deep understanding of Your promises and Your relationship with Your Creation. Amen.

God Teaches Fathers to Walk in His Light

*All Scripture is God-breathed
and is useful for teaching,
rebuking, correcting and
training in righteousness.*

2 TIMOTHY 3:16

Reading x-rays and blood lab work helps us determine our health status. And reading Scripture helps us check our spiritual health status. As we read, we can determine if we're following God's direction, trusting His promises, and remaining fit in our faith. Make these verses part of your spiritual checkup:

- "Trust in the LORD with all your heart, and lean not on your own understanding; in all your ways acknowledge Him, and He shall direct your paths" (Proverbs 3:5-6 NKJV).

- "The LORD is my rock and my fortress and my deliverer; my God, my strength, in whom I will trust; my shield and the horn of my salvation, my stronghold" (Psalm 18:2 NKJV).

- "The Spirit God gave us does not make us timid, but gives us power, love and self-discipline" (2 Timothy 1:7).

God's Word gives us direction, nourishment, and a way to measure how we are doing as men, fathers, and believers. It's a dose of what we need at just the right time.

God, give me the desire to read Your Word. May I seek Your wisdom to stay spiritually healthy. Amen.

Be Sure to Check Your Oil

The wise ones...took oil in jars
along with their lamps.

MATTHEW 25:4

In Matthew 25:1-13, we read a story of ten virgins who went to meet the bridegroom. Five didn't take oil for their lamps, and five did. When they heard that the bridegroom was coming, the five virgins without oil wanted to borrow from the others. They said no because they knew they wouldn't have enough. Let's unlock the mystery and wisdom of this passage:

- The coming bridegroom was the return of Jesus (Second Coming).
- Prudent bridesmaids were the expectant Christ followers.
- Foolish bridesmaids rejected the bridegroom and were damned.

The saddest part of this story is when the foolish bridesmaids returned with their oil to meet the bridegroom and the wedding was over. In verses 11-12 they plead, "Lord, Lord... open the door for us!" But the bridegroom answers, "Truly I tell you, I don't know you."

Don't be someone who waits too long. First Peter 3:8-22 tells you how to keep your lamp lit: Be faithful while we wait the return of Jesus, study the Scriptures, live out our lives as if Jesus was to return any time. Be a prudent man of God.

Lord, I am a man who wants to keep oil in my lamp. I want to be faithful to Your Word. Thanks for giving us Your Son, Jesus. Amen.

One Minute Alone with God Prayer

Father God, the greatest instruction manual ever written is Your Word. Yet how often do I ignore it? I ask for help over and over. I get frustrated when life doesn't go right. I pray and ask for You to show Yourself to me so that I might have greater faith. All the while, Your instruction manual and Your love letter to Your children is right in front of me. Why do I ignore the wisdom You extend to me for every minute and experience of my life?

Change me, God. Restore unto me a deep longing for Your Word and Your leading. I will turn to the Bible with hunger and with expectation of meeting You in the pages. Here, I will discover the purpose and joy You call me to. You have answered my pleas for help and answers. I'm finally ready to listen. Amen.

It's Good to Have
Your Car Washed

*Do not conform to the pattern of this world, but be
transformed by the renewing of your mind. Then you
will be able to test and approve what God's will is—his
good, pleasing and perfect will.*

ROMANS 12:2

Living near the beach, I find that my car gets dusty and
salty. When I take it to a car wash, they cleanse and polish
everything including my tires. The windows are cleaned without a streak in sight. The difference is amazing.

When we get too close to the world's dirt, our thoughts
and hearts become covered with a film of the world's grit and
grime. Here are some of the signs:

- Your heart is hardened, and you reject God's Word.
- You have become calloused.
- You have given your life over to sensuality.
- You are indifferent to impurity and greediness.

If you are experiencing any of these, you are missing out
on all that God created you to become. Don't let the world
brainwash you. Instead, offer your mind and heart to God to
be cleansed by His grace and perfect will.

*Father God, cleanse this film of the world off of me. Give me
a clear view without streaks of the life You have planned for me.
It is righteous, holy, and blessed. Amen.*

Restoration

I will repay you for the years the locusts have eaten...
you will have plenty to eat, until you are full, and you
will praise the name of the LORD your God.

JOEL 2:25-26

In American history, rural farmers have been devastated by the invasion of swarming locusts. Farmers have had to move hundreds of miles, and on occasion, they have had to find a new line of work because the locusts destroyed their way of life.

But God is a God of restoration! Even when the devastation to a human being is like the work of a swarm of locusts on a promising crop—even then, God promises to completely restore everything that has been destroyed.

The Savior's promise for Israel that we read in Joel is also a promise that you can claim for your own life. Those hard times of devastation produced by the "locusts" of your life create pathways for God to restore purpose and meaning to our lives. He gives us new peace, new joy, new goals, new dreams, and new love. What God has promised, He will do for you.

Lord, reveal to me the work You are doing. I want to catch every moment of the restoration that is taking place even now. Thank You for being the God of promises. Amen.

Just Like New

Put on the new self, created to be like God in
true righteousness and holiness.

Ephesians 4:24

The idea of being like new again is appealing. We've all had times of failure, mistakes, sin, and struggle. Yet, as much as we want to give all of this to God, we aren't necessarily sure what this new life will look like. I tell you today that becoming new in Christ is your chance to be transformed! Lay aside all the falsehood lies of the world and walk in the way of newness.

- Speak truth to everyone.
- Do not be angry (don't sin).
- Do not let the sun go down on your anger.
- Do not invite Satan into your life.
- Do not steal—get a job.
- Share with those who have a need.
- Let no unwholesome word proceed from your mouth.
- Do not give grief to the Holy Spirit.
- Put away all bitterness, wrath, anger, slander, and all malice.

With our new natures, we will be tenderhearted, forgiving each other; just as God has forgiven us. Don't miss out on fully experiencing this transformed life, my friend.

Father God, make me a new being in Your great love and grace. Give me strength to walk in the way of righteousness and faithfulness. I want to be a man transformed by Your hand. Amen.

What I Do with Money

*No one can serve two masters. Either you will hate
the one and love the other, or you will hold to one and
despise the other. You cannot serve both God and money.*

MATTHEW 6:24

In Matthew 19:23-24, Jesus said to His disciples, "Truly
I tell you, it is hard for someone who is rich to enter the kingdom of heaven...it is easier for a camel to go through the eye
of a needle than for someone who is rich to enter the kingdom of God."

What did Jesus know that the disciples didn't know? Jesus
understood that the more possessions we have, the more dis-
tracted we become from doing the work of the Lord. But I
know of many wealthy men who have kept a proper perspective. It's possible. Whether we have a little or a lot, we must
master the art of a balanced life by staying grounded in God's
Word and plan.

People who love money will do anything to get it, serving
it as their master. When God is your only master, you won't
be tempted to divide your attention and priorities.

*Lord, You are my God. Keep my focus on the things of You—
the things of eternal importance. Show me how to be a good steward of all my blessings so that I remain balanced and faithful.
Amen.*

Dollar Dos

Honor the LORD with your wealth,
with the firstfruits of all your crops;
then your barns will be filled to overflowing,
and your vats will brim over with new wine.

PROVERBS 3:9-10

Wealth is a blessing when we use it to honor God. Money should be used as a tool to serve God, not as an idol that we covet. Here are some dos to protect us:

- Know that God will provide (Proverbs 15:25).
- Repay your bills and debts with it (Psalm 37:21).
- Use it wisely (Proverbs 31:10-31).
- Give it to those in need (Matthew 5:41-42).
- Be trustworthy with it (Proverbs 11:1).
- Be an intentional giver (1 Corinthians 16:2).

Father God, I want to be a man that properly uses Your princi-
ples in handling the financial blessings You have given me. Amen.

Dollar Don'ts

By your great skill in trading
you have increased your wealth,
and because of your wealth
your heart has grown proud.

EZEKIEL 28:5

There are as many don'ts related to money as there are dos. Scripture is filled with godly advice for us to gather. Invest in God's insight and you will lead a life that is rich with faithfulness.

- Don't be jealous of those who have it (Exodus 20:17).
- Don't oppress people to get it (Proverbs 22:16; Amos 2:6-7).
- Don't hoard it (James 5:3-6).
- Don't think it will last (Jeremiah 19:11).
- Don't give special praise to those who have it (James 2:2-6).
- Don't use it for evil (Exodus 8:12-13).

Evaluate your practice of the dos and don'ts list and decide where you need to make changes. Then follow through and make the changes. You'll reap the rewards of obedience.

Father God, show me how to make the most of the resources that are a part of my life. By following Your Word's guidelines, I can be a faithful giver, receiver, and believer. Amen.

Developing Strengths
for Our Lives

To keep me from becoming conceited,
I was given a thorn in my flesh.

2 CORINTHIANS 12:7

I have good news for you! God uses the weak areas of our life to accomplish great things. There are examples throughout Scripture of this. For example, Paul recognized that God had given him a "thorn." He petitioned God three times to remove his difficulty. God answered back, "My grace is sufficient for you, for my power is perfect in weakness." With this, Paul said to himself, "I will boast all the more gladly about my weaknesses, so that Christ's power may rest on me" (2 Corinthians 12:9). Paul understood that his need made him more dependent upon God for all things.

In all of our valleys, disappointment, and sadness, a light will always be at the end of the tunnel. What is your current struggle? Spend time in prayer and in silence, considering how God is working in your situation and through your struggle. Seek His leading. He is always with us and does not leave us alone in our affliction.

Father God, You know the hurts that I have right now. Give me eyes to witness what You are doing in this. Give me a heart that praises You even as I call out for help and mercy. Amen.

Growing When You Least Expect It

This sickness will not end in death.
No, it is for God's glory so that God's
Son may be glorified through it.

JOHN 11:4

My wife Emilie's cancer diagnosis was the start of a long, difficult journey for both of us. But this trial helped us develop Christian traits we never knew were missing. During our pre-cancer and cancer treatment days, we prayed to God for a healing of Emilie's physical hardship. For several years, God didn't choose to remove it. Instead, He led us to today's verse in John.

When Emilie's health permitted, during this time she kept on recording her one-minute spots on "Keep It Simple with Emilie" on 250 radio stations, and she continued to write several bestselling books. It was amazing how God took this valley and turned it into a mountaintop experience.

If you have (or, after reading this, eventually receive) a thorn in your side, God might be asking, "So what are you going to do with it?" We may not live in a perfect world, but we do have a perfect God. Build up your faith so that when trouble occurs, you will be prepared.

God, what do I do with this trouble? How can I walk in this season of hardship with faithfulness intact? I will base my decisions on Your will and will follow where You lead. Amen.

Godly Traits Training: Part I

Whoever walks in integrity walks securely.

PROVERBS 10:9

What are some of the godly traits that are developed in this journey called life? Take a look at which ones you've learned and which you hope to learn in the near future:

- *Learn to follow directions.* Learn how to wait upon the Lord. Learn how to be still and hear His small voice through doctors, pastors, friends, leaders, and His Word.
- *Discover how to focus.* No matter what trial you're going through, you have one focus and that's to get through this period of life while keeping your focus on God.
- *Develop routines.* Major on the majors and release the minors. Priorities shape your life.
- *Build loyalty.* You'll appreciate all those who come alongside you and pray for your circumstances. You'll discover that the prayers of others are a source of great strength, especially when you have days when you aren't able to pray for yourself.

Father God, thank You for showing me through Your Word how to respond to those thorns that will appear. Amen.

Godly Traits Training: Part II

If any of you lacks wisdom,
you should ask God,
who gives generously to all
without finding fault,
and it will be given to you.

JAMES 1:5

Emilie and I continue to grow in our understanding of God, even after many years of our partnership in the Lord. Which of these traits are you learning now, and which do you need to learn?

- *Learn about follow-through.* Have the integrity to follow through. And discern when others will follow through. You will gain a deeper appreciation for the ways God is faithful.

- *Discover how to trust and who to trust.* During a valley experience, you'll learn that dependability is very important. You may need to set boundaries.

- *Learn faithfulness.* When your trial is a long one, it can be difficult to say a prayer longer than a simple one from childhood. Let those basic prayers express your heart.

- *Learn persistence.* All through Scripture, God's people were persistent in their prayers—even when it seemed like God wasn't listening. God is listening.

Father God, instill in me a passion to learn about You and Your will. I want to embrace the rich traits of the Christian life and become trusting and faithful, Lord. Teach me. Amen.

Messes Are a Blessing

The LORD gave and the LORD has taken away;
may the name of the LORD be praised.

JOB 1:21

How can anyone consider messes a blessing? Who wants to clean up those piles of unpleasant things that need to be repaired? Much of life's fulfillment is determined by how we look at things. Is our glass half full or half empty? Are we positive or are we negative about our many messes in life?

Let's see if we can turn the messes of our life into blessings simply by looking at them with new eyes and a new heart. In order for us to have dirty dishes, it means we have food to eat. Clutter means that we have possessions to share with our family and friends. Let's thank God for the abundance rather than the mess it makes.

Let's become grateful as we face the messes in our lives. The next time you are gathering the dishes or vacuuming, spend a few moments asking God how you might share from your abundance with others.

Father God, thank You for showing me that I need to be reminded that our messes are really a sign of abundance, and You are the One who so richly gives to us. Amen.

One Minute
Alone with God
Prayer

Prayer of Saint Francis

Lord, make me an instrument of Thy peace;

where there is hatred, let me sow love;

where there is injury, pardon;

where there is doubt, faith;

where there is despair, hope;

where there is darkness, light;

where there is sadness, joy.

O Divine Master,

grant that I may not so much

seek to be consoled as to console;

to be understood as to understand;

to be loved as to love;

for it is in giving that we receive;

it is in pardoning that we are pardoned;

and it is in dying that we are born to eternal life.

Thoughts to Lift Your Spirits

*Start children off on the way they should go,
and even when they are old they
will not turn from it.*

PROVERBS 22:6

For the last 15 years, I have written each of my grand-children a thought for the week to provide them with uplift-ing quotes from others, advice from me, and the strength of Scripture. It has given me an opportunity to stay connected and at the same time slowly, week after week, influence their lives with good thoughts.

Over the years, when I've visited the kids in person, I would see these notes stacked on their desk or plastered on dorm walls. Even their friends would ask to see the latest "PaPa Bob's Thought." Let me share a few with you now:

* When God solves your problems, you have faith in His abilities; when God doesn't solve your prob-lems, He has faith in your abilities.
* Let go of the past and go for the future. Go confi-dently in the direction of your dreams. Live the life you imagined.—*Henry David Thoreau*
* Be who you are and say what you feel. Those who mind don't matter, and those who matter don't mind.
* Friendship is like a book. It takes a few seconds to burn, but it takes years to write.

Father God, let me be an encouragement to those around me. I want to have a positive impact on my children, grandchildren, neighbors, coworkers, and those I meet in daily living. Amen.

Excellent Marriage Principles: Part I

Therefore what God has joined together,
let no one separate.

MARK 10:9

Over the years, Emilie and I have conducted many marriage seminars to encourage couples. The following principles are always a hit. Think about how you can incorporate them.

Really listen. Stop what you're doing and look your mate in the eyes while they speak. Then repeat back what you thought you heard them say. If you don't get it right, have them share their heart again.

1. *Laugh a lot.* One year we made it a goal to laugh every day. Try it. Be serious when you must, but try looking on the light side of daily living.
2. *Appreciate each other's good qualities.* Dwell on the positive. Compliment her new outfit or hair style. Thank her for being your life partner.
3. *Create family traditions.* Share the blessing of celebrations and family rituals. We love seeing our children and grandchildren continue traditions we started years ago.
4. *Grow your faith together.* Life is richer when a couple has a solid foundation in faith. Inspire one another to grow.

Lord, help me invest in my marriage every day by turning to Your wisdom and strength and compassion and sharing the goodness of Your heart with the woman I love. Amen.

Excellent Marriage
Principles: Part II

*Though one may be overpowered,
two can defend themselves.
A cord of three strands is not quickly broken.*

Ecclesiastes 4:12

Take one of these thoughts each day and incorporate them into your marriage.

1. *Show you care.* Go out of your way to show your wife that you love her. Help with the duties that she normally does. Get caught doing something nice.

2. *Show interest in her dreams.* Since I first met Emilie, my priority was to help her become the woman that God wants her to be. Don't be threatened by your wife's success. A lady asked me, "Do you ever feel like Emilie is in competition with you?" I replied, "No, we don't compete with each other; we complement each other." Two strands are stronger than a single strand. And when you add the strand of faith in God, you have great endurance and stability.

3. *Say "I'm sorry" easily.* A sincere apology goes a long way in healing a bad situation. Don't become petty or prideful. Ask for forgiveness when you need to.

4. *Be willing to forgive.* As Jesus has forgiven us, may we in turn be willing to forgive. In a life of marriage, sometimes you will give grace and mercy, and sometimes you will ask for grace and mercy.

Father God, You are a God of miracles. Give me a miracle in my marriage. I truly want to show her that I love her. Amen.

Be Humble in Spirit

He has brought down rulers from their thrones
but has lifted up the humble.

LUKE 1:52

Our world is full of men and women who are eager to take God's honor for themselves. But we are asked to be humble as Jesus was humble.

In the New Testament, we find the word *humility* to suggest a personal quality of dependence on God and respect for other people. It's not a natural human instinct but is a God-given virtue acquired through holy living. While the mind of the natural man is selfish and proud, the essence of Jesus' mind is unselfish and loving toward others. Christ was our great example of a proper walk. He was pleasing to God. He entered our world as a humble Savior. He became obedient to God's will, which led to His death on the cross. Throughout Jesus' walk on this earth, He taught people to be humble before God and man.

When our hearts are transformed by the Holy Spirit, we can reflect God's love to others. Humility comes from God and results in the praise of God.

Father God, give me a humble heart. As I give You honor, my life becomes a living praise to You. Show me how to step down from my throne so that I sit at the foot of Your own. Amen.

Be Afraid, but Go!

When I am afraid, I put my trust in you.

PSALM 56:3

David knew what it was like to be afraid. He was constantly running from warriors who were trying to kill him. He spent a lot of time hiding in caves to stay away from them. Nothing is wrong in being afraid. Sometimes we have to admit that we're fearful about dying, about troubles befalling our loved ones, about losing our job, about getting old, and so on.

To overcome our fear, we must first acknowledge that we do have fear. David, the psalmist, recognized his fears. "When I am afraid," he said, "I put my trust in you" (Psalm 56:3). When Emilie was little and afraid to move around the house at night, her mother's advice was "Be afraid, but go." Emilie believed her mother and took the steps of courage to face her fear. To this day, we often tell our kids and grandkids "Be afraid, but go!" It is great advice.

Admitting your fear and still going forward will help remove the fear out of fear.

Father God, let my trust in You overcome the fears that I have. I've trusted You in the past, I trust You today, and I'm going to trust You for the future. Amen.

Play by the Rules

Whoever finds their life will lose it, and whoever
loses their life for my sake will find it.

Matthew 10:39

In golf, out-of-bounds markers are throughout the course. If we go out of bounds, we're given an added stroke to our total. In tennis, game points and matches are lost when that yellow ball goes beyond the white line.

The rules are set. Consequences happen when those rules are broken. But people don't want to play by the rules, and they don't want the consequences to breaking them. Yet God has outlined in His Word certain moral boundaries we are to live by. Those who obey them will be blessed, and those who do not listen will not receive the blessings from God.

God did not give these boundaries to take away all of our fun but to enjoy His blessings by keeping them. Moses says to Israel in Deuteronomy 30:19, "I have set before you life and death, blessings and curses. Now choose life in order that you and your children may live." God wants us to make wise choices to live by. His boundaries are good for us.

Father God, I can give witness that Your boundaries have been good for my life. You have given me more blessings than I ever thought I would have. Thank You! Amen.

Sexual Love

*Husbands, love your wives, just as Christ loved
the church and gave himself up for her.*
EPHESIANS 5:25

Scripture uses two verbs for love: *phileō* and *agapaō*.
Ancient Greek has words for sexual love—the verb *eraō* and
noun *erōs*—but neither of those occur in the New Testament. Nevertheless, Scripture does talk about sexual love. We
can feel sexual desire toward a person. This type of love has a
very strong appeal. Men (because they are more visual than
women) need to mark this as a "red flag." Sexual love certainly
has its place in a marriage relationship. But sexual love, if not
discriminately used, can control your life. This form of love
needs to be controlled *by* you. Men…be patient.

Males tend to go from sexual love to *phileō/agapaō* love,
but females often develop *phileō/agapaō* love first and then
go to sexual love. Your wife or girlfriend might say, "He grew
on me!" She developed sexual love *after* getting to know you
as a friend. Even after marriage, never forget this need of the
woman in your life. She wants you to be her number one
friend of the opposite sex.

*God, You created a physical, passionate love for a husband
and wife to share. Help me show my wife how much I adore her
by being a man who remains honorable, attentive, and loving.
Amen.*

Phileō Love

Finally, brothers and sisters, rejoice!
Strive for full restoration,
encourage one another, be of one mind,
live in peace.

2 CORINTHIANS 13:11

Often referred to as friend love, *phileō* love is the kind you share with a close friend. *Phileō* love can be extended to your next-door neighbor or anyone you know really well.

This love is extremely important in finding your life mate. Friendship is the foundation for a healthy marriage. Unlike sexual love, *phileō* love is developed as you begin to know and value a person's character traits and interests. You should have *phileō* friends of your gender. Men tend to be loners, but I encourage guys to have several other friends. If you're a married man, be careful with ladies who want to be friends. We all need to have acquaintances, but we also must guard our hearts when it comes to having friends of the opposite sex.

I develop *phileō* love with my wife when we go on picnics, hike, watch movies, or share a bag of popcorn. Our wives and our other *phileō* friends bring out the best in us. We love to be around them. They help civilize and inspire us.

Father God, give me male friends who support my desire to be a man of integrity. And show me how to nurture phileō *love in my marriage with daily effort. Amen.*

Agapaō Love

You shall love the Lord your God with all your heart,
and with all your soul,
and with all your mind,
and with all your strength.

MARK 12:30

The noun *agapē* and verb *agapaō* are the most common words for love in the New Testament. This love actively sacrifices personal feelings and needs to meet the needs of the other person. It is *agapaō* love that makes you rise above yourself and meet the needs of your spouse at the end of a tiring workday.

To allow *agapaō* love to infuse and rule the other two dimensions of love in our lives, we must first know and submit to Jesus Christ as our personal Savior. This basic commitment is a prerequisite to moving beyond sexual and *phileō* love. It is God's will for Christians to allow *agapaō* love to dominate all of their relationships, bringing more depth and love to marriage. *Agapaō* love is the foundation of a relationship committed for life.

You can also have *agapaō* love for people to whom you are not married. Your children, your parents, your fellow Christians can all experience an *agapaō* love with you.

Father God, let my mind go beyond my thoughts regarding the word love. *Let me experience all three forms of love. I want to go deeper in what I presently experience. Amen.*

One Minute Alone with God Prayer

Jesus, You walked the earth among men, as a man. You experienced the trials and temptations and joys that I experience. Time has passed. The world has changed. And yet, when I study Your life and look to it as my example to follow, nothing is missing. Nothing is lacking. The brilliant way You taught people continues to enlighten. The compassion You showed the "least of these" remains a call to love and kindness. And there isn't a day that goes by when I don't need to hear echoes of Your corrections of leaders, teachers, and believers who were so focused on the law that they forgot about loving their neighbors and remaining devoted to You and You alone. An ongoing relationship with You, the Savior and living Lord, means that I can walk with You today. I can learn from You. I can sit at Your feet. And I can be touched by Your healing hand. Thank You, Jesus. Your eternal presence transcends time and circumstances and allows me to be with my Lord right here and now. We face this life together, and I will walk in Your ways with gratitude. Amen.

Pageant of the Masters

*We are God's masterpiece, He has
created us anew in Christ Jesus,
so we can do the good things he
planned for us long ago.*

EPHESIANS 2:10 NLT

We live near Laguna Beach, a small town on the Pacific coast of California that puts on a wonderful, annual world-famous event called "The Pageant of the Masters." During this show, the community presents a live rendition of a masterpiece painting. They capture the scene in the painting perfectly. They don't change it or move, and they present a live version of the image designed by the master painter.

Paul the apostle tells the people of Ephesus that God has transformed them from sinners into a masterpiece. How does God make us into His masterpiece?

Paul tells the Christians in Corinth they are a new creation: "If anyone is in Christ, the new creation has come: The old has gone, the new is here!" (2 Corinthians 5:17). God changes you from a sinner to His child through His grace. God's in the restoration business, and He wants you to become a child of God and become one of His masterpieces.

Father God, You are a healer of man's sins. Help me realize that I don't have to remain as a sinner, but I can become one of Your great masterpieces. Amen.

Be in the "In" Crowd

Trust the Lord forever, for in Yah, the Lord,
is everlasting strength.

Isaiah 26:4 nkjv

Regardless where we live, some people are always trying to be in the "in" crowd. We don't just experience this as children in school—we can also experience it as adults. When cliques exist, you are either in or out. And the answer is often determined only by material matters, such as income level, physical appearance, your career, and so on.

When we take on the wisdom of Scripture, we have the strength and direction we need to go beyond the clique stage of life. We have the chance to expand our future and hope by serving and caring about the community of believers. This is that deep *agapaō* love in action. When your focus becomes self-centered *or* centered on what other people think of you, turn your thoughts toward the friend, the neighbor, or the stranger that God brings to your path today.

Remember it is not your strength as a Christian but Christ *in you* that gives you value, purpose, and meaning. Those who give themselves to God's work are the true "in" crowd.

Father God, help me to look beyond myself so that I serve You and others. I want to be able to honestly tell others that my life is not about me but is about Christ in me. Amen.

Your Value Through Grace

For it is by grace you have been saved,
through faith—and this is not from yourselves,
it is the gift of God—not by works, so
that no one can boast.

EPHESIANS 2:8-9

The harsh world and sometimes even your own self talk can tell you that you are worthless, stupid, or a failure. You might think you'll never amount to anything. In contrast, God tells you that you are loved, you are redeemed, and you are forgiven. Paul vividly describes what our lowly status was in Ephesians 2:1-3. Then he tells us of the marvelous remedy of God (verses 4-22). Through the grace of God, we have become...

- alive with Jesus
- raised with Jesus
- seated at the right hand with Him in heaven
- the masterpiece of God's creation

"Therefore, there is now no condemnation for those who are in Christ Jesus, because through Christ Jesus the law of the Spirit who gives life has set you free from the law of sin and death" (Romans 8:1-2). Paul assures us that you are undoubtedly free in Christ. Rest in this freedom and in your great value through the eyes of God.

Father, I want to experience the full freedom of salvation. When other voices tell me that I'm not worthy of love or forgiveness, remind me of my worth as a new creature in Christ. Amen.

Be a Man of Integrity

Teach me to do Your will, for You are my God;
Your spirit is good.
Lead me in the land of uprightness.

PSALM 143:10 NKJV

I often hear this cry: "Where have all the good men gone?" We cry out for leaders in all fields that show leadership, courage, and integrity. Many prominent personalities have fallen from grace because they've acted out on emotion rather than with reason and spiritual strength. Sometimes only one big misstep causes them to tumble. As soon as it becomes public, these men would give anything to be in that moment and rethink their behavior and choices and priorities.

We must continually be on guard to make sure our motives are pure and that our priorities are those of God. When we are spurred on to make selfish choices, we lose self-respect, and we have missed the mark of God's great plan for us. Take each step and make each decision with a reverence for God's Word and His purpose in your life. Don't let yourself become a man who spends a lifetime regretting that one moment in time.

Father God, hold me back from selfish actions so I don't hurt my family, friends, coworkers, or my future in Your will. Lead me to a life of integrity. Amen.

Know God's Ways

Show me your ways, LORD; teach
me your paths. Guide me in
your truth and teach me, for you
are God my Savior,
and my hope is in you all day long.

PSALM 25:4-5

Living out God's truth by living a life of integrity requires knowledge of God's ways. Here are some verses to meditate on. Become familiar with God's path of righteousness:

- "Guard my life and rescue me; do not let me be put to shame, for I take refuge in you. May integrity and uprightness protect me, because my hope, LORD, is in you" (Psalm 25:20-21).
- "I will sing of your love and justice; to you, LORD, I will sing praise. I will be careful to lead a blameless life...I will conduct the affairs of my house with a blameless heart" (Psalm 101:1-2).
- "The integrity of the upright guides them, but the unfaithful are destroyed by their duplicity" (Proverbs 11:3).

God, You show me the way in which to walk. Give me the strength to follow Your commands. I want to recognize the significance of each action, choice, word, prayer, and path. Amen.

Knowledge in Motion

*Blessed is the one who does not walk
in step with the wicked,
or stand in the way that sinners take or
sit in the company of mockers,
but whose delight is in the law of the LORD,
and who meditates on his law day and night.*

PSALM 1:1-3

From the verses we've explored related to integrity and others from Scripture, we can understand how faithfulness relates to how we conduct ourselves in godly ways. In other words, sitting in our overstuffed chairs watching TV doesn't produce integrity. We have to put our knowledge into motion:

- Know His ways.
- Learn His path.
- Behave in an upright manner.
- Delight in and meditate on the law.
- Sing of lovingkindness.
- Walk in righteousness.

Be a man of action. Don't sit back and hope that your life will be one of integrity. Invest in the rewarding and transforming labor of becoming a man who pleases God in all that he does.

Father God, give me motivation to put my desires into action. I have to focus every day on how I will respond in certain situations. I want to be a man of courage. Amen.

Fitting Together the
Puzzles of Life

*I appeal to you, brothers and sisters, in the name
of our Lord Jesus Christ, that all of you agree with
one another in what you say and that there be no
divisions among you.*

1 Corinthians 1:10

I've been on a five-month journey to change my eating lifestyle. So far I've lost 37 pounds. As I sift through my closet, I pull out a shirt or pair of pants—hold it away from me and say, "Too long, too short, too big, too small, too tight." I'm in search of a piece that fits.

Finding a church that "fits" poses similar problems. We get itchy to change churches when one thing doesn't suit us. The worship is loud, the pastor is too old, the pastor is too young, the sermon is light on theology, and so on. In Ephesians 2:22, Paul tells us we are "being built together to become a dwelling in which God lives." Take the gifts and talents that God has given you and be an encouragement to those in your church. It's amazing how soon you realize that you "fit" as soon as you start reaching out.

Father God, show me the church where You can use me. Let me reach out and use my gifts and talents in service to You and always with praises on my lips. Amen.

The Power of One

Serve one another humbly in love.

GALATIANS 5:13

During Jesus' ministry, He dealt with large crowds of people, but He never lost sight of the importance of time spent with one person. Here are several of those intimate times:

- His conversation at night with Nicodemus (John 3).
- Visiting a woman at the well in Samaria (John 4).
- Talking with Zacchaeus in the sycamore tree (Luke 19).

On the morning of our daughter's sixteenth birthday, when she was old enough to date, she even received a dozen red roses from a certain sincere young man who had waited patiently for a chance to date her, but he did not know Jesus. Over the first nine months that they dated, we had many evenings getting to know him and sharing our faith. One Sunday evening, the young man joined us for the service of music at a nearby church. To our surprise, at the altar call at the end of the service, this young man walked down the aisle and accepted Jesus. Don't ever doubt the importance of connecting with one person—Jesus never did.

Father God, let me be willing to be used one-on-one if that is Your desire for me. I don't want to underestimate the value of one person. Amen.

Be an Encourager in Life

Do not let any unwholesome talk come out of your mouths, but only what is helpful for building others up according to their needs, that it may benefit those who listen.

EPHESIANS 4:29

The words we choose to use begin to define us. Most movies and daily conversations these days are filled with language that wasn't acceptable in my youth. Little thought is given to how these word choices are destructive to both the speaker and the hearer.

In today's verse, Paul warns the early church to not let negative words come out of our mouths. What comes out of the mouth begins in the heart. He wisely calls us to use words that (1) build up another person, (2) are appropriate for the moment, and (3) are a blessing to the hearer.

A guiding principle in our family is, "You never have to apologize for words you never say." Any words spoken need to be covered in love.

"You're great! You've got talent! You play the piano so well! Have you ever thought to go out for the football team?" These are all edifying words. They may not sound powerful to you, but the hearer says, "That's someone who likes me."

Father God, protect my heart so I won't store up unkind words or thoughts. Let my speech be affirming to the listener. Amen.

Drive-Thrus Not Allowed

Hope in the LORD, and keep his way,
He will exalt you to inherit the land.

PSALM 37:34

In my younger days, McDonald's, Burger King, and Taco Bell didn't exist. We would sit down at the local diner and share a meal and fellowship for an hour or two, sometimes just catching up on the local news.

We thought nobody would ever want to speed up a process we considered to be so enjoyable. Clearly, we weren't good prophets! Not only did fast food restaurants become popular, but they became even faster with the advent of a drive-thru window.

Our spiritual, physical, and emotional health requires time spent with family, friends, and God. Drive-thrus are not allowed when you invest in what matters most. When you spend time and attention on godly priorities, you'll discover that life tastes so much better.

Father God, slow me down. Help me to see what needs my attention today. Align my priorities with Your own. Show me how to invest in You and the people of my life with my time. Amen.

One Minute
Alone with God
Prayer

Father God, You made me in my mother's womb, and You know about every part of my life. You created me to walk in fellowship with You and to serve You by walking in my purpose. Reveal to me the next step I am to take. Burden my heart with those concerns and hopes I need to lift up in prayer. And this heart You placed inside of me is made to extend grace, love, patience, strength, and hope to others. I know that I am only able to do this when I trust the leading of the Holy Spirit within. Help me to follow this leading for every decision and in every area of my life.

There isn't one valley or one mountaintop moment I've experienced that You have not witnessed and been a part of. Thank You for coming alongside me and showing me what it means to live as a godly man in every season. Amen.

How to Meditate

I meditate on your precepts and consider your ways.

PSALM 119:15

Meditating on God's Word is a lost discipline in our culture. What does it even look like?

As a young boy, I lived on a small farm in New Mexico. We had 14 milk cows. When they went into the pasture, I observed them eating grass and chewing and chewing…all day. Dad explained they were chewing their cud. The cows filled their stomachs with grass and then brought it back up to chew it some more. A bit gross to consider, but by doing this important, deliberate process, these cows provided healthy milk for the town folks.

When we meditate on God's Word, we are, in a way, "chewing our cud." In Psalm 119 we read David's view of taking in and processing God's Word and experiencing the healthy results of meditating: We combat sin (verse 11), we find delight in His Word (verses 15-16), we find valuable truths (verse 18), we find favors in living daily (verse 24).

Meditating is going deeper than the words on paper; it is going deep so we can change how we live. It's the mirror image of a cow chewing her cud. As we chew on God's truths, they provide health and healing for our lives.

Father God, let me take time to read and study Your Scripture. I don't want to be in a hurry. Let it fill me and flow through me so that I produce the fruit of meditating on Your Word. Amen.

Parenting Principles: Part I

*Children are a heritage from the LORD,
offspring a reward from him.*

PSALM 127:3

When you're a parent, eyes are always watching you to see if you do what you say you believe. Read Psalm 127:1–128:4 to discover good parenting principles.

Create a godly foundation. "Unless the LORD builds the house, the builders labor in vain" (Psalm 127:1). The people of the Old Testament knew they needed protection from the enemy, but they also knew that their ultimate security was the Lord standing guard over the city.

Be still and listen to God. We rise early and retire late, but the psalmist tells us that these efforts are futile (Psalm 127:2). Take time to hear God's leading for you and your family.

Take care of your children. In verse 3 we read that children are a heritage from the Lord. In the Hebrew, "heritage" (*nakhalah*) means "property, possession, inheritance." Truly God has loaned us our children to care for and to enjoy for a certain period of time. Raising children takes time, care, nurturing, and cultivating. The cost is worth the results.

Father God, I pray that my children see a man of God and a father of love and conviction when they watch my life. Give me a heart that extends extra compassion, patience, and wisdom for the sake of my dear family. Amen.

Parenting Principles: Part II

*Watch yourselves closely so that you
do not forget the things your eyes
have seen or let them fade from
your heart as long as you live.
Teach them to your children and
to their children after them.*

DEUTERONOMY 4:9

God has entrusted to you some very special people—your children. You will be held accountable for how you take care of them, but you are not in it alone. God offers these guidelines and so many more in His Word. Keep studying Psalm 127:1–128:4 to see what God is teaching you.

Become wise and skillful. Insightful parents know their children's unique abilities and needs. Psalm 127:4-5 talks about how parents are to handle their offspring.

Make the Lord a priority. God is central to a home's happiness (Psalm 128:1-2).

Let God be the source of life, beauty, and meaning. The Lord will be a source of beauty and life in the home (Psalm 128:3).

Seek God's blessing. With the Lord's blessing, children will flourish like olive trees, which generously provide food, oil, and shelter for others (Psalm 128:6).

What areas do you want to ask God for strength and improvement?

Father God, forgive me for times when I shortchange my family. Teach me how to be a good father and show me what it takes to make our home a place of safety, strength, and love. Amen.

Think Small

Know this love that surpasses knowledge—
that you may be filled to the measure
of all the fullness of God.

Ephesians 3:19

We're often told to "think big!" I'm from Texas, and growing up, I always heard, "Everything's bigger in Texas." People felt bigger was better. But when it comes to spiritual matters, small is big to Jesus:

- "You have so little faith. Truly I tell you, if you have faith as small as a mustard seed, you can say to this mountain, 'Move from here to there,' and it will move. Nothing will be impossible for you" (Matthew 17:20).

- "Whoever can be trusted with very little can also be trusted with much, and whoever is dishonest with very little will also be dishonest with much" (Luke 15:10).

- "And if anyone gives even a cup of cold water to one of these little ones who is my disciple, truly I tell you, that person will certainly not lose their reward" (Matthew 10:42).

Are you willing to focus on the small things and give them value? Jesus did.

Father God, there are so many examples of You working miracles through everyday people and events. May I be willing to see Your big love and purpose in the smallest of moments and experiences. Amen.

Find Rest for Your Souls

Come to me, all you who are weary and burdened,
and I will give you rest.

MATTHEW 11:28

Many times Jesus is spending time with the ordinary people, the sinners, the poor, the people with health problems, and people who had social issues. Jesus was always appealing to the downcast, the poor in spirit. He didn't ask them to instantly rise to being the CEO of their company, the starting quarterback of an NFL champion team, a brilliant scientist, or the lead pastor of a mega church. Instead, He beckoned them in their weariness and said He'd give them rest. How often do we receive such a loving offer of help and comfort?

God's call to you is not an invitation to "do more" or become greater in the world's eyes. God's call is an invitation to find rest, comfort, and help. It is an open offer to continually be filled up. Isn't that an incredible thought? The source of the deepest, greatest strength is right in front of you as you enter God's presence. Make time today to stand before the Lord and be filled.

Jesus, You call me to You because You see how much I need Your help and strength. You fill me in ways that things of the world cannot. I want to be dependent upon You for my every need. Amen.

Give Your Burdens to God

*Take my yoke upon you and learn from me, for I am
gentle and humble in heart, and you will find rest for
your souls. For my yoke is easy and my burden is light.*

MATTHEW 11:29-30

Jesus' yoke involves instruction under discipline. But it's
easy. So as I live life and see many decades pass, I can verify
that grace is much easier on one's life than the law. This passage also reveals a lot about Jesus: He is gentle, humble, willing to give rest for your soul, and His load is light.

The load of the world is heavy. Our sins weigh us down
and our desire for possessions or status feels like an anchor.

Large, trained oxen are tame and gentle. We watched
them at a local agricultural event. One of the farmers directed
his oxen with only a short wand that weighed less than eight
ounces. The farmer guided the two big animals with gentle
direction.

Might and weight are not required when you follow the
will of the Lord. Turn to Jesus today to find a peace that will
refresh your body, mind, and soul.

*Father God, who of us doesn't need Your rest and peace. Let me
learn to be still and know that You are God. Amen.*

What to Do with Time

Be very careful, then, how you live—not as unwise but as wise, making the most of every opportunity, because the days are evil.

EPHESIANS 5:15-18

Our verse today challenges us to approach our time with wisdom and godly discernment. We need to see each day as an opportunity to serve Him in ministering to others and walking in His will.

The big, meaningful mystery of living is, "How do I know the will of God?" You'll find help uncovering the answer by reading Scripture, praying, consulting with friends who have shown wisdom in formulating life decisions, and listening to the Holy Spirit—then be willing to take one big giant step in the direction God is leading. If you're not properly hearing His leading, He'll send you in another direction.

Following the will of God is harder than knowing the will of God. So stay devoted to prayer. Use your time wisely by asking God for the strength to follow Him every minute.

Father God, guide me in my day so that I discern Your will and have the courage to follow it. I want to be wise and godly. Show me what You have planned for me today, Lord. Amen.

Good Advice

Go to the ant, you sluggard;
consider its ways and be wise!

PROVERBS 6:6

Here are some ideas that might give order to your days and peace to your soul and life.

1. Never borrow from the future. If you worry about what will happen tomorrow and it doesn't happen, you have worried in vain. If it does happen, you have to worry twice.

2. Pray daily.

3. Get at least eight hours sleep each day.

4. Get on a regular schedule so you won't have to rush into the day.

5. Say "no" to good things, and save your "yeses" for the best.

6. Delegate those tasks to others that you don't need to do.

7. Live a simplistic life that unclutters your life.

8. Live by this life principle: Less is more.

9. Allow plenty of time between two appointments.

10. Do first things first. Don't lump hard things together.

Practice one of these principles today and another one tomorrow.

Father God, may I hold onto helpful principles in my life. I know it will give me more time to be with You. Amen.

Remaining Humble in Success

You have too many men. I cannot deliver Midian into
their hands, or Israel would boast against me, "My own
strength has saved me."

JUDGES 7:2

We live in a culture that screams out, "Me, me! It's all
about me! I accomplished this, and my resources and skill
and speaking ability have provided all that I have." When we
hear such words of praise for oneself, we can guess that, given
enough time, that man or woman will fall. God wants us to
be dependent on Him in all things.

In Judges 7:2, our verse for today, God said to Gideon,
"You have too many men. I cannot deliver Midian into their
hands, or Israel would boast against me, 'My own strength
has saved me.'"

God was asking Gideon, "Who do you trust, Me or the
size of your army?" In essence that is what God asks us as men,
"Who do you trust?" We must depend upon God, not the size
of our army, our possessions, our power, our bank account,
how many homes we own.

Father God, release me from any pride that restricts me from
acknowledging Your power in my life. All that I have, all that I
am, and all that I have been able to accomplish is through Your
grace alone. Amen.

"Do You Love Me?"

What good will it be for someone to gain the whole world, yet forfeit their soul? Or what can anyone give in exchange for their soul?

MATTHEW 16:26

Men, our society wants to make us feel good for what we wear, where we live, the size of our estate, or how much power and influence we have. We think the more we can consume, the more success we have. If we have all these things, but do not have our soul right with God, we have nothing.

All God wants to know from you and me is the answer to the same question that Jesus asked Peter: "Do you love me?" (see John 21:15-17).

Even though our material possessions make us feel safe, they can be gone in an instant. But God's strength and His plan will never fall away. Do you sing His praises when others praise you? Do you give God the glory when someone gives you credit? God isn't examining your resume in order to understand your worth, but He examines your heart. Is your heart ready to be reviewed?

Father God, when I stress about the world's view of me, remind me that You examine my heart to discover my value. Help me lead my family by example by professing my love for You often. Amen.

One Minute Alone with God Prayer

God, old habits are hard to break. As I spend more time with You, I become aware of the actions, behaviors, decisions, patterns, and temptations that I want removed from my life. I can't do this without Your strength and discernment. Show me how to make lasting changes. Fill me with desires that are designed for me by You. I need to persevere right now. When I'm frustrated, Your grace covers me. When I stumble, I need not quit the race out of shame. I will return to the ways You have shown me, and I will keep my eyes fixed on You as I press on.

I am grateful to have a new vision for what my life can become as Your son. It inspires me, in turn, to show my family and others what being transformed by faith and Your love looks like. The process of renewal can be slow, but I will hold tight to my purpose in You. Amen.

Grace Is the Word

He said to me, "My grace is sufficient for you,
for my power is perfected in weakness."
Therefore I will boast all the more gladly about
my weaknesses, so that Christ's power may
rest on me. That is why, for Christ's sake,
I delight in weaknesses.

2 CORINTHIANS 12:9-10

In one of the apostle Paul's letters, he says he has a thorn in his side. This probably isn't a physical thorn. Rather, it is more likely a struggle of some kind. Paul understands that this difficulty remains so that he will not exalt himself. Paul realizes and later expresses that his weakness becomes a vessel for God's strength! Can you view your weakness in this way? Do you receive God's grace as your strength in that area of limitation? I've always shared that the word *grace* is...

G—God's
R—riches
A—at
C—Christ's
E—expense

What areas of your life are you still trying to perfect in your own strength? Release those to God's grace. Experience the riches of God working through you, through Christ.

Father God, may I take the time to realize that all of my blessings come from You. It's not by my power, strength, or might. You are the provider. Amen.

Soul Friends

After David had finished talking with Saul,
Jonathan became one in spirit with David,
and he loved him as himself.

1 SAMUEL 18:1

One of the most difficult tasks for men is to make solid friendships. Unfortunately, we've perceived or been taught that we have to rely on ourselves. Friends and associates will disappoint us, so suck it up and rely on your own power. In 1 Samuel 18, 19, and 23 we discover a great example of friendship in the deep relationship between Jonathan, the king's son, and David, a shepherd boy. They accepted each other, even though socially they were far apart. David and Jonathan exhibited several traits that are found in friendships:

- Unconditional love
- Personal enjoyment
- Mutual interests
- Mutual acceptance
- Mutual commitment
- Mutual loyalty

These two men from different backgrounds depended on each other's strengths to shore up their individual weaknesses. To be a friend, you must be involved in the other person's life. It takes time and commitment to be a friend. You have to be willing to put your friend's needs above your own.

Lord, help me become a better friend to the men in my circles. Reveal to me someone who can be a Jonathan or a David in my life. I want the gift of friendship that You bring into our lives. Amen.

A Father Who Trusts

The L ord is near to all who call upon him,
to all who call upon him in truth.

Psalm 145:18

When we become dads, we know that we need help. But sometimes we get ahead of ourselves and think that we have to be responsible for every move we make and every decision that is made that impacts our child. Out of a desire to be strong and honorable, it is possible to lose sight of God. A father is a man who not only hears God's Word, but who also lets it penetrate into his heart and soul. We need men who will give testimony to what God means in their everyday lives. A godly father can be trusted because he has endured the tests of the world and has been found true to Christ's calling.

Talk to your child and tell them what it means to you to be a father and a believer. Share with them all your prayers and hopes for their lives and futures. Invite your child to pray with you. Show them exactly who you go to for your every need.

Father God, reveal to me the ways in which I can be a stronger example of Your love and strength as a father. And remind me to always direct my child's eyes and heart to You. Amen.

Two A.M. Friends

Confess your sins to each other and pray for
each other so that you may be healed.
The prayer of a righteous person is
powerful and effective.

JAMES 5:16

When we moved into our present neighborhood, we met a great couple who lived down the street. One day I saw the husband painting his front picket fence. To get to know him better, I strolled down in paint clothes to offer my help. It blew him away—few people in Southern California even know their neighbors, let alone offer to help a neighbor in need. We've become very close since then, praying for one another through health and life journeys.

"Two a.m. friends" (as I call them) are the people you can call early in the morning with a prayer need or to ask for help. They are also the friends you gladly take a call from in the wee hours. These special friends are the ones who have been great supporters for me during times that I didn't want to be transparent about some of my lows. Don't miss out on the great gift of such a friend. Be willing to pick up the phone—no matter what time it is!

Father God, thank You for bringing my two a.m. friends into my life. I can't imagine where I would be without them. Amen.

Keep Your Ways Pure

How can a young person stay on the path of purity?

Psalm 119:9

Young man, old man, we all struggle with purity. In Psalm 119, David continually had such a struggle, giving us 11 principles to defend ourselves from the darkness:

1. We should listen to Your Word (verse 9).

2. We should seek Your heart (verse 10).

3. Let me not wander from Your commandments (verse 10).

4. Let me hide Your Word in my heart so I won't sin against You (verse 11).

5. Praise be to You, and teach me Your statutes (verse 12).

6. I fall in love with everything that comes from Your mouth (verse 13).

7. I fall in love with all the stories revealed in God's testimonies (verse 14).

8. I will meditate on Your precepts (verse 15).

9. I will follow them (verse 15).

10. I will delight in Your statutes (verse 16).

11. I will not forget Your Word (verse 16).

David reminds us that God's Word is essential for our lives.

Father God, give me the desire and heart to build Your purity in my own life. Surround me with men who will give me support in that desire. Amen.

Remembering PaPa's Prayers

Devote yourselves to prayer, keeping alert in it
with an attitude of thanksgiving.

COLOSSIANS 4:2

A couple of years ago, every time I took a step it hurt. So one day I went to the doctor. With x-ray in hand, he declared to me, "Mr. Barnes, it's all in your knees!"

For a moment, the doctor's words really took me back. When I was ten, we would visit my grandfather, a Nazarene pastor. Every night, we knew that PaPa would lead us in a very lengthy prayer while we knelt in front of the sofa. He seemed to pray for everyone in the world. At the end of the 45 minutes, my knees hurt so badly. I'd go to bed in pain.

In the denomination in which I was raised, we didn't get on our knees to pray. I realized that even if I'm not on my knees to pray, how often do I pray? This Colossians 4:2 passage tells us to continue earnestly in prayer.

Whether we are on our knees, standing up, or seated, do we pray continually in all of our situations? We can find help from many sources—friends, counselors, books, church—but there's nothing better than the support and strength we get from God when we pray.

Father God, I thank You for all the godly influences in my life. Amen.

More Good Advice

*Therefore, my dear brothers and sisters, stand firm. Let
nothing move you. Always give yourselves fully to the
work of the Lord, because you know that
your labor in the Lord is not in vain.*

1 CORINTHIANS 15:58

Going to Scripture often, seeking wise counsel, and praying for God's renewal can transform us. Here's advice for daily living:

1. Live each day to the maximum.
2. Learn to let go of concerns that are not yours.
3. Never spend more than you can earn.
4. Learn to KMS (Keep Your Mouth Shut). You don't have to apologize for something you never said.
5. We all are kids inside; do something for yourself daily that is childlike.
6. Read something uplifting and spiritual each day.
7. Learn about nutrition and eat healthy each meal.
8. Select a place for everything and learn to put everything in its place.

You never know what message you need to hear and when. But God does!

*Father God, give me an ear for good and godly advice. And
help me become a man who is grounded in Your Word and wisdom so that I pass along honorable advice to others. Amen.*

A Friend Who Goes
the Extra Mile

When they could not find a way to do this because of the crowd, they went up on the roof and lowered him on his mat through the tiles into the middle of the crowd, right in front of Jesus.

LUKE 5:19

In Luke, there is a great story of friends who carried their lame friend on his bed to a house to see Jesus. The crowd prevented them from going through the door, so they climbed up some outside stairs with the sick man on his bed onto the roof to lower the man and his bed inside the home near Jesus. I can just hear the dialogue that went on between the friends:

- This will be fun—like a party.
- We can't tear into a roof.
- The debris will fall down on top of Jesus.
- Who will fix the roof when we're finished?

Fortunately, the friends hadn't spent time debating who would fix the roof. They just earnestly wanted to get their friend healed. That is a big question: "How much do we love our friends?" Or do you sit back and ask, "But who will fix the roof?"

Father God, may I be willing to bring a friend to Jesus. I want my heart to ache for my friends who do not know who You are. Amen.

"Get Up"

He said to the paralyzed man, "I say to you,
get up, take your mat and go home."

LUKE 5:24

You can imagine the amazement that Jesus and those in the crowd experienced as they saw the crippled man being lowered through the roof. Some could have thought...

- The nerve of them.
- Escort them out!
- Make them wait in line and take their turn like we did.

But when Jesus saw the man, He didn't scorn him or his friends: "When Jesus saw their faith, he said, 'Friend, your sins are forgiven'" (verse 20). Some of the scribes and Pharisees were very upset: "Who is this fellow who speaks blasphemy? Who can forgive sins but God alone?" (verse 21).

Jesus replied, "'I want you to know that the Son of Man has authority on earth to forgive sins.' So he said to the paralyzed man, 'I tell you, get up, take your mat and go home.' Immediately he stood up in front of them, took what he had been lying on and went home praising God."

What is God asking you to do? What is He healing you of?

Father God, You welcome me into Your presence. You never scold me for my awkward ways or struggles. Thank You. Amen.

How Good Is Good Enough?

"Teacher...what must I do to
inherit eternal life?"

LUKE 10:25

Many of us ask ourselves, "How good is good enough?" Jesus had a disagreement with the religious leaders about this very thing. They were always telling the people how much they needed to do to get back in God's good grace. A scribe asked Jesus the question posed in our verse today. Jesus responded by asking the scribe how he reads the law.

The scribe correctly answered, "'Love the Lord your God with all your heart and with all your soul and with all your strength and with all your mind'; and, 'Love your neighbor as yourself'" (Luke 10:27). The scribe then wanted to know who his neighbor was (verse 29).

Jesus answered with the parable of the Good Samaritan, explaining that we're not just to love those who love us. In fact, we're to love our enemies, do good to them, and lend to them without expecting repayment. Jesus also taught these things earlier in Luke 6:32-35.

So how much is enough? Jesus took all our sins to the cross and died for us. And now, He gives us His free grace. And when God shows you who your neighbor is, you are to love that person with His great love.

Father God, let me expand my vision on who my neighbor might be. Let me open my eyes that I might see. Amen.

One Minute
Alone with God
Prayer

Father God, I want the character and integrity I need to become a leader. I've tried the world's devices to rise up. There is the corporate ladder. There is the accumulation of money. There is networking and gaining popularity as a way to rise in status. But I want my ability to lead to be shaped from within. I want my source for wisdom and discernment to be You and You alone. Keep me humble, Lord. Show me how to become a man of God who waits with patience to be shaped, molded, and refined.

Give me a godly mind and heart so that I am a steward of the many responsibilities You have given to me: family, faith, work, home life, friends, serving others. There is no need for me to look any further. Each of these is vital in Your eyes. When I want to conquer the world, remind me that a real leader leads right where he is. I am here. Use me, God. Amen.

Even More Good Advice

Better the poor whose walk is blameless
than a fool whose lips are perverse.

PROVERBS 19:1

1. Use your commute time to fill your mind with good things. Listen to thoughtful radio talk shows, uplifting music, or good audiobooks. Libraries have great free selections of these. And you can find numerous audio presentations of the Bible.
2. God says, "Be still and know that I am God." Schedule quiet time each day.
3. Make friends with godly people.
4. Learn to laugh a lot.
5. Be a serious worker, but learn to give yourself grace.
6. Be positive when dealing with others. We have enough critiques in this world.
7. Learn and practice the art of forgiveness.
8. Remember, there is no "I" in TEAM.
9. Learn to slow down and smell the roses.
10. Every night before bed, thank God for all the blessings He has given you that day.
11. Don't worry. Eighty-five percent of the things you worry about never happen.

You see? Wisdom doesn't have to be long-winded and filled with complicated rules. Small efforts come with big rewards in the Christian life.

Father God, give me the strength and awareness to make small and consistent godly changes in my life. Amen.

Be a Road Builder

*"Make level paths for your feet," so that the lame may
not be disabled, but rather healed.*

HEBREWS 12:13

One summer we decided to drive from Southern California to visit some friends who had rented a delightful home in Brookings, Oregon—a small, charming seaside community. The 900-mile drive up the beautiful California coast was on a two-lane highway through the massive redwood forest. I thought of all the people, planning, and heavy equipment required to create this road up countless hills and around many curves.

As Christians, we're building roads for the next generation to follow. Our faithfulness very likely will determine how difficult or smooth their journey will be. The writer of Hebrews warns the people to make straight paths so that the people traveling them won't stumble over troubles but rather will experience healing. As the next generation walks on the road you have built over your lifetime, will they thank you for helping prepare them for life, or will they blame you because you weren't good stewards of taking care of the path and roads that God gave you?

Father God, You have given me this stretch of road to care for. It is my life and my life's journey. Help me be a good steward by shaping smooth pathways of Your truths for those who follow. Amen.

We Are the Church

Trust in the LORD forever, for the LORD,
the LORD himself, is the Rock eternal.

ISAIAH 26:4

As I pass by the churches in our area, I'm always thankful for the ones who went before us, to make today's church to be alive and well. We must never forget what it cost in time, effort, and finances to make everything we value so much, such as our colleges, hospitals, government, freedom, clear air, clean water, and so on. Every blessing is because someone invested in these priorities.

Remember, you are part of the church. What you do as a believer is an extension of the body of Christ. When you are moving forward in the direction of God's will, you are taking the church to the places God is calling you to.

What do you want your part of the church to be about? Are you a trainer, teacher, or leader? Are you a small chapel welcoming people into a sanctuary of silence and prayer? Are you a missionary, reaching out to others at home and abroad to expand the kingdom? You are the church. How will you bless others and the work of God today?

Father God, I forget that I am part of the body of Christ and the church. Help me step fully into this exciting role. I want to be the church. Amen.

Money Matters That Matter

*You must never think that you have made yourself
wealthy by your own power and strength. Remember
that it is the LORD your God who
gives you the power to become rich.*

DEUTERONOMY 8:17-18 TEV

God holds us accountable to faithfully manage our resources for Him. To do this, we must develop wisdom and self-control. Major money mistakes are…

- *Going in debt.* Romans 13:8 tells us, "Let no debt remain outstanding, except the continuing debt to love one another."
- *Living a money-centered life.* Matthew 6:21 says, "Where your treasure is, there your heart will be also."
- *Trying to get rich quick.* "Those who want to get rich fall into temptation and a trap and into many foolish and harmful desires that plunge people into ruin and destruction" (1 Timothy 6:9).
- *Withholding benevolence from those who need help.* "A generous person will prosper; whoever refreshes others will be refreshed" (Proverbs 11:25).

Become a good steward. It is a learning process that requires time, attention, and faithfulness.

God, my possessions are not to serve me but to serve good purpose, You, and others. Help me rid my life of those things that rule my time and my attention in negative ways. Amen.

Your Mighty Creator

*This is what God the LORD says—the
Creator of the heavens, who stretches them out, who
spreads out the earth with all that springs from it, who
gives breath to its people, and life
to those who walk on it: "I, the LORD,
have called you in righteousness."*

ISAIAH 42:5-6

From the first chapter of Genesis, we read these things of God's creations:

- He created light and separated the waters.
- He created heaven.
- He created day and night.
- He created dry land—earth.
- He created the seas.
- He created plants, vegetation, trees.
- He created evening and morning.
- He created living creatures.
- He created man.

The amazing Creator crafted the heavens and the earth and you. Take everything before God. He will form great things from the struggles, emptiness, and doubts we offer up to Him.

Creator, when I question how You could possibly work in the midst of my great trial or change my heart or life, Genesis reminds me of Your amazing ability. You are an awesome, loving God. Your ability and strength is beyond anything I could ever conceive. Amen.

Filled Up

For God was pleased to have all his
fullness dwell in him.

COLOSSIANS 1:19

In Ephesians 5:18-21, we receive Paul's description of what the believer should look like when they are filled with the Holy Spirit. Consider whether you exemplify these qualities and traits:

- Don't be drunk with wine.
- Be filled with the Holy Spirit.
- Speak to others in psalms, hymns, spiritual songs.
- Sing and make melody with your heart.
- Always give thanks for all things.
- Be subject (submissive) one to another.

Which of these are missing from your life or seem rather troublesome? Is it difficult to imagine speaking to others in psalms? Consider memorizing Scripture and sharing it with your wife as a way to encourage her. Ask the Holy Spirit to fill you and lead you every day.

Father God, thank You for the gift of the Holy Spirit. I want to be filled and then overflowing with all the joy and grace of the Spirit. I am so grateful that You provide me with leading. Amen.

Partnership

*The Lord God said, "It is not good
for the man to be alone.
I will make him a helper suitable for him."*

Genesis 2:18

Christian marriage is a parallel portrayal of Christ and the Church. We're only able to submit to another person in marriage when we first are able to submit to Christ, the head of the Church. As men, we are to be willing to become a servant to our wives. We are to respect, honor, and lead them in a strong walk with the Lord. God created them to be our helpmate. (God knew we would need someone to help us out.)

Many couples make wedding vows they aren't willing to keep. The view is that if it doesn't work out, they can divorce. But marriage is more than a marriage license; it's a covenant we make to God. Men, we are made to be a servant. Just as Jesus came not to be served, but to serve. If we love, love, and love some more, we will be respected by those we love.

Father God, as Jesus came to serve, I want to do a better job in how I serve my wife, family, and those around me. Amen.

When You Want to Ask "Why?"

God is our refuge and strength,
always ready to help in
times of trouble. So we will not
fear when earthquakes come
and the mountains crumble into the sea.

PSALM 46:1-2 NLT

It seems to be very human to ask this "Why?" question when disaster strikes. Our inquiring minds want to know. Why would a loving God permit such destruction, devastation, and death? The sad fact is, we live in a fallen world, and events happen according to the laws of nature. Because of the sin of mankind there will always be things that happen other than what we would want. There will be trouble and suffering beyond our control. At such times, our comfort must come from God's Word.

In today's verse we find three comforts: 1) God is our refuge, 2) God is our strength, and 3) God is always ready to help in times of trouble. If we can internalize these "big three" promises we can live life with victory.

Father, give me a heart that turns to Your comfort and refuge and promises each time I face a trial. I know I don't live in a perfect world, but I serve a perfect God. I'm so grateful. Amen.

What's Number One?

One thing I ask from the LORD,
this only do I seek:
that I may dwell in the house of the
LORD all the days of my life.

PSALM 27:4

Do you sometimes feel like you're on a merry-go-round? We are going in circles at a great rate of speed, and we're not sure how to get off.

Multitasking seems to be the catchword of this decade. If we aren't able to juggle a lot of balls at one time, we will probably fail in whatever pursuit we attempt. How can one narrow the priorities down to just one? Not many of us even want to have just one thing to focus on. However, this was David's request when he asked the Lord for just one thing: "That I may dwell in the house of the LORD all the days of my life, to gaze on the beauty of the LORD and to seek him in his temple."

That's what our focus should be. Get off the fast track and narrow our focus on priority number one. We all know what we should do, but our character won't always give into our heart's desire.

Father God, give me one thing today to focus on. Give me a sole desire in my heart so that I can remain true to what You call me to do. Amen.

Be Transformed

Take delight in the LORD,
and he will give you the desires of your heart.

PSALM 37:4

Have we been so neutralized in our heart that we can't hear the voice of the Lord when He speaks to us? Our culture has a way to numb us in our souls. One of my favorite verses reminds me where my heart should be: "Do not conform to the pattern of this world, but be transformed by the renewing of your mind. Then you will be able to test and approve what God's will is—his good, pleasing and perfect will" (Romans 12:2).

That is my battle cry: "Don't be conformed, but be transformed!" We each have our own struggles and demons. It makes me think of playing tug-of-war as a kid. When the coach would yell "Go," each team would pull and pull until we had no strength left in our arms. That's the way life is, but instead of people pulling against each other, we are pulling against principles. These two principles are called "conformed" and "transformed." The one with the strongest pull in your life will win the game of life. We have to decide which one is the desire of our heart.

Father God, give me the courage to make the right choices of life. Give me the added strength to fend off the enemy. Amen.

One Minute
Alone with God
Prayer

God, I am struggling to make time for You and Your Word. The days get so busy, and my mind gets cluttered by all these needs, demands, and objectives. More often than not, I end up feeling buried by responsibilities. I'm losing the joy of faith. Help me straighten out my priorities so I know what can be cleared from my life. Give me the courage and commitment to make my time with You a priority.

God, forgive me for the times I encourage my family toward busyness. Forgive me for checking email and watching television instead of interacting with the people right in front of me. And forgive me for making excuses instead of being with You, listening for Your leading, and talking to You. Give me the desire to spend more minutes alone with You. Amen.

Remember the Great
Moments of Life

*But Mary treasured up all these things
and pondered them in her heart.*

LUKE 2:19

As I get older, I reflect upon the past and take great joy in the sweet memories and blessings:

- How fortunate I was to live with Christian parents.
- When I became a believer in Jesus on Easter Sunday as a 12-year-old.
- When I chose Emilie to be my wife.
- When God blessed me with two children, Jenny and Bradley.
- When he gave me three wonderful careers: school teacher, manufacturing of factory-built housing, and a writing and speaking career.
- The birth of our five grandchildren.
- The birth of our first great-grandchild, Emi Ianni.
- The miracle in healing Emilie from cancer.

In our church there is a communion table with these words carved in the wood: "This do in remembrance of me." Celebrate the memories of triumphs, trials, and joys; and make special memories for your family.

Father God, don't let me forget the many blessings that make up my past. Guide me in the direction of Your will so that I walk in the way of more memories crafted by You, Lord. Amen.

Find Your Target

*Trust in the LORD with all your heart and
lean not on your own understanding;
in all your ways submit to him, and he
will make your paths straight.*

PROVERBS 3:5-6

As a man, a husband, a father, and maybe even a grandfather, are you living life with a clear purpose? If not, why not? If we don't have a target, we won't know if we hit the target. President Abraham Lincoln had a wonderful goal for his time as president: "I desire so to conduct the affairs of this administration that if at the end, when I come to lay down the reins of power, I have lost every other friend on earth, I shall at least have one friend left, and that friend shall be down inside of me."

Unfortunately, he wasn't able to see that desire fulfilled, but history remembers that he was a man who lived his short life not only for himself, but for others and for his convictions.

We all leave a legacy that others will remember us by. If there is but one thing you leave as a legacy for others to follow, let it be this: "He was a man who trusted God."

Father God, I set my focus on You and Your purpose for me. Help me stay true to You as I live with integrity and honor. Amen.

What to Put On First

Therefore, as God's chosen people,
holy and dearly loved,
clothe yourselves with compassion, kindness,
humility, gentleness and patience.

COLOSSIANS 3:12

Fashion is more popular now than ever before. Models, fashion designers, and retailers are vying for your attention to sell their version of fashion. But God isn't concerned with your outerwear—He only cares about the character that adorns your heart. In today's verse, we read of five characteristics a man should have in his spiritual wardrobe:

- a heart of compassion
- kindness
- humility
- gentleness
- patience

Paul wrote the letter to the Colossians because he was concerned about the false teaching that was being preached. He wanted to make sure that the true believer was properly clothed with the proper inward elements and character. He wanted to stress that the real believer stood out from the nonbeliever. Are we any different than the rest of the world? Be sure these traits are what you put on each day. Let your godly characteristics shine.

Lord, You have changed my heart. Give me the desire to clothe my heart with the right characteristics. I need help in all of these areas. Give me strength. Amen.

Spiritual Wardrobe: Part I

God opposes the proud but shows
favor to the humble.

JAMES 4:6

Too often we have a tendency to blend in to the secular men around us. Those around us might say, "I didn't know he was a Christian. He seems like he is like the rest of us." Wouldn't that be a shame? Let's take a closer look at the characteristics we should put on as Christians. Here are three of the pieces in our spiritual wardrobe. Are you wearing them today?

- *Compassion.* Empathy allows you to be aware of others' distress and develop a desire to alleviate that distress. Are you a man who is willing to help those in need?

- *Kindness.* More than good manners, kindness is about helping an older person with a heavy load, comforting a child, assisting your wife with a project, and watching for opportunities to extend God's love with words, actions, and prayers.

- *Humility.* When you wear humility, you are a team player. In fact, others are more important than you. Humility lets you pull your ego out of the way so that you can help others.

God, show me when, where, and how I can put on godly character. I look forward to extending myself and my heart with more conviction and commitment to Your will. Amen.

Spiritual Wardrobe: Part II

Clothe yourself in honor and majesty.

JOB 40:10

Keep going through that internal closet of your heart. What else is there when you follow God with the power of grace and the covenant of commitment?

- *Gentleness.* People love to be around gentle people. They feel safe and are more likely to let their guard down. A gentle person makes a good friend. To me, the gentle man is the opposite of the angry man. Gentleness attracts, and anger causes one to flee to a safer harbor.

- *Patience.* In our hurried-up world, we tend to veer away from patience and even from situations that require us to be patient and quiet. I've always been considered a patient man, but I really learned patience after spending many hundreds of hours waiting in a doctor's office or hospital during Emilie's cancer treatments. The hard times will break you or make you more patient.

We've now explored five godly characteristics. Are you living them? When these are evident in our lives, then people around us will know something's different about us—who knows, they may even ask you, "There's something different about you. What is it?"

Father God, You have challenged me to look at these five areas of my life. I want to improve in each area. Help me to become the man You want me to become. Amen.

I Am the Clay

"Can I not do with you, Israel, as this potter does?"
*declares the L*ORD*.*

JEREMIAH 18:6

"Hope deferred makes the heart sick, but a longing fulfilled is a tree of life," says Proverbs 13:12. Disappointments are God's appointments. God uses setbacks to renew our focus on Him and to strengthen our faith, giving us new opportunities. I know this to be true. Emilie and I were giving seminars and writing books on home organization, godly marriage, and how to be effective parents and grandparents. But in 1997, cancer gave us new opportunities to guide others through this new valley in our life. We could share about holding onto faith throughout the cancer journey.

If you find yourself in some very difficult valleys of your life, stop searching for all the answers in the wrong places. Seek God. Our theme verse through these last 12 years has been John 11:4: "This sickness will not end in death. No, it is for God's glory so that God's Son may be glorified through it."

Father God, thank You for giving me a new opportunity to serve others because of the things I'm learning today. Let me realize that others will be able to learn through my disappointments. Amen.

Be a Home Builder

By wisdom a house is built, and through
understanding it is established;
through knowledge the rooms are filled
with rare and beautiful treasures.

Proverbs 24:3-4

We are a nation that is seeking to have success in raising a healthy family. Everywhere you turn, there is advice on how to raise healthy children. In many cases, you can pull up a few good ideas, but Scripture is very clear: Life should be lived in dependence on the Lord and that children be regarded as a heritage from the Lord. This wonderful verse reveals what we need to be blessed as a family: wisdom, understanding, and knowledge.

- *Wisdom.* In the book of Proverbs, Solomon writes so that the reader might know wisdom and allow it to govern their life.
- *Understanding.* We need to not only read the Scriptures but let the Word sink into our brains so that we give thought to what is being taught until we comprehend the principles.
- *Knowledge.* Knowledge doesn't happen by accident. It requires effort on our part.

Father God, thank You for giving me the proper insight in raising our family in Your ways and not in the ways of the world. We are blessed! Amen.

She Touched Me

You shall know no God but Me;
for there is no Savior besides Me.

HOSEA 13:4 NKJV

We have all sung the great hymn, "He Touched Me," but in my case, *she* touched me. My elderly Sunday school teacher, when she saw that I was a little hesitant to stand with the other boys to proclaim my faith in Jesus, leaned around the back of the other classmates and tearfully looking straight in my eyes said, "Would you like to rise with the rest of the boys?" She put her hand under my elbow and lifted me up just a little bit, and I nervously stood on my own two feet. I walked very carefully forward to the front of the church to meet my pastor with the others. That same evening, I had the honor to be baptized.

I have never forgotten it was my teacher who influenced me to take a stand. That was the very best decision I have ever made in my life. You may be beyond the eighth grade, but maybe you need to make the same decision. Today you can stand wherever you are and accept Jesus as your very own Savior.

Father God, I thank You for that Sunday school teacher who was so interested in me that she gently touched me that Easter morning. Amen.

Job—the Hero

*In all this, Job did not sin by charging
God with wrongdoing.*

JOB 1:22

The book of Job wrestles with the age-old question: Why do righteous men suffer, if God is a God of love and mercy? It clearly teaches the sovereignty of God and the need for man to acknowledge such. Job's three friends gave essentially the same answer: All suffering is due to sin. Elihu, however, declared that suffering is often the means of purifying the righteous. God's purpose, therefore, was to strip away all of Job's self-righteousness and to bring him to the place of complete trust in Him.

Through all of his tragedies, Job remained God's man. He showed us how things on the outside can be taken away from us, but no one can take away those things on the inside.

What will we do when the things of life are taken away from us? What will happen to the inner man? Will we stand strong in Christ? Do you cling to circumstantial hope and belief? Or is your faith one that will endure? Grow your trust in God every day.

Father God, what a story of character about a man who was faithful to You when everything went bad. What a model he is to all of us men. Amen.

Time for God

I will call on Him as long as I live.

PSALM 116:2

You know you should spend time with God each day, but time glides by so fast, you aren't able to squeeze in just a few minutes. Have you ever really considered what God wants to give you during these daily times together?

Paul writes in Galatians 5:22-23, "The fruit of the Spirit is love, joy, peace, forbearance, kindness, goodness, faithfulness, gentleness and self-control." These—along with guidance, wisdom, hope, and a deeper knowledge of who He is—are what God wants to give to us during that sacred time together. These nine big character builders are to be learned throughout your life. I've been working on these areas for over 50 years and I barely have made a dent on my list, but I'm getting better every year.

"But," you say, "Who has time? My to-do list is always longer than my day. When could I find even a few minutes to read the Bible or pray?" Let me answer your questions with a question. Are you doing what's important in your day—or only what is urgent? General Dwight Eisenhower once said, "Emergencies are usually not important, and if it's important, it's usually not an emergency." The successes of life are often determined by the choices we make based on the priorities we've set. Make time for God this week.

Lord, help me discern what is most important each day. Help me recognize and remove any obstacles that keep me from spending time with You. Amen.

One Minute Alone with God Prayer

Lord, I am bombarded by nuggets of information and ideas all day long. It is easy to embrace them as they come or to quickly dismiss them, even when they are important, because I am busy and don't want to be bothered. But I want to be a man who compares all that comes my way to Your truths and assurances. I want to process every claim, comment, and declaration through the filter of Your Word. Give me the discernment to ignore what isn't important or true. Give me the wisdom to take in and reflect on those ideas that are of You and are a part of my path in Your will.

I'm listening, Lord. I'm ready to have my eyes and heart open to Your leading every step of the way. Grant me a patience that can endure the chaos of this world. I want the steadiness of my salvation and the foundation of my faith to become my sources of strength. Amen.

Do You Really Believe?

So you are no longer a slave, but God's child;
and since you are his child,
God has made you also an heir.

GALATIANS 4:7

You may have heard that God loves you and wants to spend time with you, but do you really believe it? It's true. The God of the universe wants to be with you, His child (John 1:12; Galatians 3:26). He created you, He loves you, and He gave His only Son for your salvation (John 3:16). Your heavenly Father has chosen to be with you. Now you must choose to be with Him.

When you're alone with God, I suggest that you read and dwell on God's Word. Find encouragement in devotional books and in teachings from godly leaders. Then spend time in prayer.

A men's group at church can be a source of great encouragement. Or maybe a couple coworkers would like to meet up for lunch once a week to check in with each other about the faith journey? Find a way to make time for God. He can't wait to spend these moments together.

Father God, I want to create space in my day to sit with You and to read Your Word. Connect me with other men who long to nurture a deeper Christian walk. Amen.

Renewed Spirit

I will give them an undivided heart
and put a new spirit in them;
I will remove from them their heart of
stone and give them a heart of flesh.

EZEKIEL 11:19

We put a lot of stress on our hearts. Some of that stress is caused by unhealthy food, high pressure lifestyles, and lack of physical exercise. Other health problems can stress our hearts as well.

Spiritually speaking, we are all born with a congenital heart problem—sin. We are all sinners and prone to rebel against God's plan for our lives. The more we press on in our own way, the more damaged our hearts can become. Our hearts become hardened when we turn from God's Word and His hope. But there is renewal and healing for us sinners. God promises that He will give us a new heart and a new spirit through salvation. We are able to replace our hardened old heart with a new one that beats for God's best and expands to take in love, grace, and hope.

To take advantage of this wonderful opportunity, all you have to do is surrender your heart to Him. Why wait?

Father God, Your Word is true. Let wisdom reign in my life as I put my trust in You. I long to have a renewed heart and spirit. Amen.

How to Talk to God

I call on you, my God, for you will answer me;
turn your ear to me and hear my prayer.

PSALM 17:6

The more you talk to God, the more comfortable it will feel. Talk to God as you would to your earthly parent or a special friend who loves you. Here are some ways to start the dialogue and keep it going with God.

- Thank God for all He has done for you and for all He is doing for you.
- Confess your sins. Tell God about those things you have done and said and thought for which you are sorry.
- Pray for others' physical, emotional, and spiritual needs. Ask God to work in the heart of someone you hope will come to know Jesus as Savior.
- Pray for yourself. Ask God to help you do His will so you can serve Him throughout the day (Philippians 4:6).

Spend time alone with God in the morning, and you'll start your day refreshed and ready for whatever comes your way. Spend time alone with Him in the evening, and you'll go to sleep resting in His care and wake up ready for a new day to serve Him.

Father God, give me a yearning to get to know You better. May my prayers be a conversation with You. I thank You for wanting to be with me. Amen.

The True Source

*All Scripture is inspired by God and is useful for
teaching, rebuking, correcting and training in
righteousness, so that the servant of God may be
thoroughly equipped for every good work.*

2 TIMOTHY 3:16-17

Americans seem to always be in search of the secret to life.
Lifestyle media is the favorite place to look. Even at the grocery store we are bombarded with paperback books and magazines that show some celebrity who gives their secrets for success:

- How to lose 15 pounds in 30 days.
- How to find your soul mate.
- Seven safety tips for your next vacation.
- No more worries, no more cares.
- Thirteen crazy ideas that sometimes work.

Over the years, I have found that all of my questions about living life are answered in God's Word. As a young man I had a pastor who often said these words: "If God said it, that settles it." Don't keep searching when you have the source of God's instruction and the expression of His heart right in front of you.

Father God, forgive me for how often I look for my answers elsewhere. You invite me and direct me to come to You for knowledge, truth, and next steps. I will look to You alone. Amen.

Don't Keep Worrying

*Do not set your heart on what you will
eat or drink; do not worry about it.*

LUKE 12:29

When we realize we can't control every little aspect of life or the big situations, we tend to worry. Instead of feeling relief that God is in control, we start to figure out ways to take on everything and resolve all the troubles. This only gets us into trouble and steers us away from the peace of the Lord.

We have a saying in our home: "Wednesday is set aside for worrying." You know what? When Wednesday comes, all the things that we had on our worry list had already been resolved.

When you're tempted to place your trust in yourself rather than in God's power and plan, turn to this verse and regain your trust in the Lord. "'I know the plans I have for you,' declares the LORD, 'plans to prosper you and not to harm you, plans to give you hope and a future'" (Jeremiah 29:11).

Father God, thank You for being in control. I don't have to have all the answers; I only need to know You are the One who shapes my today and my future. Amen.

A New Creation

If anyone is in Christ, the new creation has come.
The old has gone, the new is here!

2 CORINTHIANS 5:17

Have you ever tried to shake up your life by taking on a new, healthy habit? Did you stick with it? It is possible to transform by releasing old behaviors and adopting new ones. If you do something for 21 consecutive days, you can create a new habit. We must realize that we no longer want to be as we have been, but are made to be new creations in Christ. Since the day I met Jesus, I realized that I no longer wanted or liked my old self. It wasn't about discontentment with my life. This desire to be made new was motivated by my longing to become the man God intended me to be.

Becoming a man of God begins with making a personal commitment to Jesus Christ. Only He can give us the strength to change. Only He can give us the fresh start that allows the spirit to grow strong in us. That's what I discovered many years ago! My life began to change from that moment on and the years since then have always been an exciting adventure.

Father God, I realize that change is possible. Give me the strength to change so I am more like You. Amen.

Time to Move On

*There is a time for everything, and a season for every
activity under the heavens.*

ECCLESIASTES 3:1

Why spend so much energy looking back at life and wondering "what if"? Repeating something from the past so that you can do it better, more perfectly, or more lovely is a nice thought, but none of us are granted do-overs in this life. As much as I might like to go back to certain seasons of my life and adjust decisions I made in younger years…I can't do it. No one can—so stop looking back. What's done is done. God has placed each one of our lives on a timeline, with a specific beginning and a specific end.

We can't go back and we can't stand still. We can move forward in the plans God has for us. We can know that we have the peace and security of God's love and His grace and mercy.

So yesterday is yesterday and today is today, and life must be lived with faith and in God's great abundance, joy, and purpose in the 24 hours directly before us.

Lord, please lead me forward when I'm stuck in the past or in the mire of my mistakes. I want to live this moment for You and invest in a future shaped by Your grace, not by my past sin. Amen.

Things Not Seen

Now faith is confidence in what we hope for and
assurance about what we do not see.

HEBREWS 11:1

We can worry, we can be sorry for our past, or we can live by faith. It's your choice. Over the years we have known people who have lived choice number one and choice number two. That's not the life I want to live. And God wants so much more for all of us. But to embrace God's best for us and the assurance of things hoped for, we need to live by faith. Memorizing verses about faith can become your biggest source of strength for your life:

- "It is by grace you have been saved, through faith— and this is not from yourselves, it is a gift of God" (Ephesians 2:8).
- "Trust in the LORD with all your heart and lean not on your own understanding" (Proverbs 3:5).
- "Since we have been justified by faith, we have peace with God through our Lord Jesus Christ" (Romans 5:1).

Choose faith each day of your life. Rest in God's hope and truth as you lead your family, encourage others, and walk in purpose.

Father God, let me be wise in how I will live my life. Let me live a life that my legacy will be, "He was a man of great faith." Amen.

The Power of the Cross

The message of the cross is foolishness
to those who are perishing,
but to us who are being saved it
is the power of God.

1 CORINTHIANS 1:18

Many people around us think that we who depend on God and His Word need some crutch to get through life. I will usually ask those people, "And what is your crutch?" Faith in Jesus is not a crutch: it is a source of power.

Paul calls the message of the cross "the power of God"— and Scripture presents that message. "Power" is a translation of the Greek word *dunamis*, which our English word "dynamite" comes from. Anyone who considers God's Word to be useless will eventually experience the full impact of God. When our grandson Chad was seven, he and his friends were talking about who Jesus was and is. When one friend said he thought Jesus was just a good teacher, our grandson said, "Richard, that's not going to cut it." I was so proud that Chad knew that the message of the cross is a message of eternal power. May we all be as wise and as willing as this young man to speak up.

Father God, thank You for inspiring Your holy Word. It has changed my life and the lives of millions around the world. May it continue to set men free. Amen.

One Minute
Alone with God
Prayer

Father God, I will walk forward in this day with the intention of listening for Your voice and watching for Your guidance. Some days I start out with this plan, but then I lose my focus as soon as the busyness takes over. Father, I want to follow Your lead. When there are distractions, I will cling to Your side. I will lean in to hear what You have to say. I will be patient when You are showing me the way of Your will. I want to live each day this way, God.

As I grow closer to You, I will discover how to live a life of integrity, character, honor, strength, faith, and righteousness. I will discover how to be a whole man of God. Amen.

Wait on the Lord

Since ancient times no one has heard,
no ear has perceived,
no eye has seen any God besides you,
who works for those who wait for him.

ISAIAH 64:4

Often many sports fans have been so discouraged by their team's performance that they left early to beat the traffic and did not realize that their team had won at the last second! We often stop short of spiritual blessings as well. Consider God's view of pressing on and facing your life with endurance and patience:

- "The race is not to the swift...but time and chance happen to them all" (Ecclesiastes 9:11).
- "Do you not know that in a race all the runners run, but only one receives the prize? Run in such a way as to get the prize" (1 Corinthians 9:24).

When we step into God's presence and wait with patience, we receive the strength and direction we need to run the mighty race He has for us. Don't give up before the finish line. Don't quit before the innings are all played. God is working in you even now.

Father God, forgive me for my impatience. It stops me from resting and walking in Your will. Give me a heart that is willing to wait and then to run this race of life with endurance. Amen.

Learning Curves

Wait for the Lord; be strong and
let your heart take courage;
yes, wait for the Lord.

PSALM 27:14 NASB

My learning curve for learning to wait upon the Lord came after my wife, Emilie, was told she had cancer. In that instant, our world of convenience came to a halt. Health issues suddenly became our top priority. For 15 years, we've had to adjust our expectations to embrace our new version of life, complete with delayed doctor appointments, countless hours in the waiting room, painful procedures, and more.

As soon as I figured out that the adjustment was all about my impatience, I slowly was able to wait and even learn through the inconveniences. Throughout Scripture we read where the men who walked with God were the ones willing to wait on God. I soon came to the conclusion that if I wanted to wait, I had to draw closer to God. We have to be willing to wait on the Lord to receive His many blessings. You will discover, as I did, that there is great wisdom and grace in the waiting.

Father God, may others not have to learn to wait on You while they are going through a valley in their life. May we all learn at an early age to trust You in every aspect of our life. Amen.

What Do You Chase After?

When I surveyed all that my hands had done and what I had toiled to achieve, everything was meaningless, a chasing after the wind; nothing was gained under the sun.

ECCLESIASTES 2:11

Our society tells us that we have value or status only if we have accumulated a lot of things. In Ecclesiastes 1:2, Solomon had this to say about such efforts: "Vanity of vanities; all is vanity" (KJV). In today's verse, we are given a look at Solomon's wisdom about all his human efforts to acquire and achieve. He saw them as elusive pursuits because it is God who gives our lives meaning and value.

Paul understood the ultimate principle for successful living. He expresses it very well when he says, "To me, to live is Christ and to die is gain" (Philippians 1:21). Our life is through Christ and Christ alone. Through good times and bad times, through sickness and health, through the up times and down times, we need to express joy—because God has saved us from our sins.

Can we as men stand before God and call out "For me to live is Christ"?

Father God, give me the faith that I might be able to say with excitement and dedication, "For me to live is Christ." Amen.

My Peace I Give You

Peace I leave with you; my peace
I give you. I do not give to
you as the world gives. Do not let your
hearts be troubled and do not be afraid.

JOHN 14:27

If we walked down the busy sidewalks in the world and asked the people what their number one desire for the world would be, a large majority would reply, "I would love for everyone to live in peace!" But not many people really pursue peace in the world.

So what was Jesus talking about when He said He would give us peace? "Do not suppose that I have come to bring peace, but a sword" (Matthew 10:34). This seems startling, doesn't it? After all, didn't Jesus say that he would give us peace? Jesus was presenting the idea of embracing God's kingdom, which can cause strife because it opposes man's version of a kingdom or of power.

We all long for peace to unfold in difficult situations in our lives and throughout the world. But true, lasting peace is that which Christ gives you within. Let this peace guide you, change you, and change the world around you.

Father God, Your peace is an everlasting peace. When I make it about politics or power, remind me that change needs to happen within my heart. I want to be transformed. Amen.

A Surprise Gift

*All things come from you and from
your hand we have given you.*

1 CHRONICLES 29:14

One day an elderly grandmother came to the White House and asked to see the then president, Abraham Lincoln. The receptionist asked the busy president if he had time to welcome this woman into his office. As was Lincoln's style, he graciously consented. As she entered his office, he rose to greet her and asked how he might be of service. She replied that she had not come to ask a favor. She had heard that the president liked a certain kind of cookie, so she had baked some for him and brought them to his office.

Emotional, the president responded that she was the first person who had come to his office without intending to ask *for* something but rather to give him a gift.

Think of giving God a gift. Nothing pleases our heavenly Father more than our sincere thanksgiving. Surprise Him today with the gift of pure worship and praise.

Father God, let me continue to be a vessel that gives. I am so thankful for all Your gifts to me and my family. May we, in turn, give back to You a portion of that love. Amen.

Good Old Cowboy Advice

If any of you lacks wisdom, you should ask God,
who gives generously to all and without finding fault,
and it will be given to you.

JAMES 1:5

As a young boy, I remember going to town on a Saturday afternoon with Dad and PaPa. After being treated to a five-cent ice cream cone, I would sit on a bench in front of the county courthouse and listen to all the great wisdom of the farmers and cowboys. Here are just a few of the one-liners they would utter:

- Forgive your enemies. It messes up their heads.
- When you wallow with pigs, expect to get dirty.
- Live an honorable life so when you're older and think back, you'll enjoy it a second time.
- Don't interfere with somethin' that ain't botherin' you none.
- If you find yourself in a hole, the first thing you do is stop digging.
- Good judgment comes from experience, and a lotta that comes from bad judgment.

The cowboys didn't have a lot of book learning, but they were able to see life in its basic form and were able to express it in everyday language. Learn to be simple with your words.

Father God, continue to give me more than just knowledge. I want to be more than that. I want to take knowledge and turn it into wisdom. Amen.

Remarkable Spirit

If the Spirit of him who raised Jesus from the
dead is living in you, He who raised Christ from
the dead will also give life to your mortal bodies
because of his Spirit who lives in you.

ROMANS 8:11

The Gospels reveal incredible stories about people meeting Jesus and being transformed forever:

- A leper approached Jesus and asked Him to heal him from his terrible disease. Jesus reached out His hand and touched the leper and said, "I am willing…Be clean!" And the leper was healed immediately (Matthew 8:2-3).

- Jesus healed Peter's mother-in-law of her fever. Then she got up and waited on Him (Matthew 8:14-15).

- When on a rough sea, the crew became very scared. Jesus spoke to them and said to them, "Take courage! It is I. Don't be afraid" (Mark 6:50).

- When Jesus was at the pool in Bethesda, Jesus said to a man who had been lame for 38 years, "Get up! Pick up your mat and walk." Immediately the man took up his pallet and walked (John 5:1-9).

Lord, the Spirit of Him who heals the sick and replaces fear
with absolute peace is the One who has changed me forever.
Thank You, Almighty God. Amen.

How Full Is Your Glass?

But may all who search for you be filled with joy and gladness in you. May those who love your salvation repeatedly shout, "The Lord is great!"

Psalm 40:16 nlt

As one looks at a half glass of water, they will either consider it half full or half empty. It can't be both. A positive person, an optimist, will say it's half full and the negative person, a pessimist, will think it's half empty. I try to stay away from the half-empty crowd; they seem to drag me down. I'm naturally more upbeat, and I like to stay positive.

When we read in Scripture to "be filled up," it means to continually be filled up. We don't just have one filling, but we are continually and consistently being filled. We do that in many ways: We can read God's Word, we can pray, we can be polite to someone who cuts us off on the freeway, we can be givers to God's work, we can be still and know that He is God.

Father God, fill me up. Give me the eyes and heart of a half-full person so that I can receive Your goodness in full measure and give that to others as it flows through me. Amen.

Keep Filling Up

*For the earth will be filled with the knowledge
of the glory of the LORD.*

HABAKKUK 2:14

God's Word is full of half-full statements. All the way from Genesis to Revelation, we read of statements that are affirming:

- "God created mankind in his own image, in the image of God he created them; male and female he created them" (Genesis 1:27).
- "Now go; I will help you speak and will teach you what to say" (Exodus 4:12).
- "Love your neighbor as yourself. I am the LORD" (Leviticus 19:18).
- "I will be glad and rejoice in you; I will sing the praises of your name, O Most High" (Psalm 9:2).
- "I will sing of the LORD's great love forever" (Psalm 89:1).
- "He has made us to be a kingdom and priests to serve his God and Father—to him be the glory and power forever and ever. Amen" (Revelation 1:6).

Father God, I want to be a person with an attitude that reflects the hope I have in Your promises. Amen.

A Man of God

Be on your guard; stand firm in the faith;
be courageous; be strong.

1 CORINTHIANS 16:13

No one ever said that being a Christian man would be easy. Paul realized that in AD 90 when he wrote the church in Corinth—by the way, he didn't have an iPhone or iPad. He didn't even have the Western Union to send his letters. He wrote them on crude paper with slow drying inks. Then he had to find a dependable courier to hand carry these morsels of truth. He made great effort to encourage the men of the church. He inspired them and inspires us today with his call to:

- Be alert.
- Stand firm in the faith.
- Act like men.
- Be strong.

To have a strong footing in your identity as a man of God, reclaim the four principles Paul describes.

Father God, I want to be a man as Paul encouraged the men in Corinth. I want to be a man of God. Amen.

One Minute
Alone with God
Prayer

Jesus, when I examine Your life and death and resurrection, I know that I am being asked to follow You, my Savior, with the courage to live in a way that is pleasing to God. My job on this earth and in this lifetime is not to please the world or to reach a predetermined level of success. My role is to have fellowship with You and to listen for Your leading and then walk in Your will. Jesus, when You spoke to the spiritual leaders of Your day, You did not conform to their faulty teachings to please them. Instead, You spoke wisdom and truth and You shed light on the false instruction so that God's promises and power would be illuminated.

Even when You were busy, You paid attention to the infirm, the children, the widows, the outcasts. Everything about Your ministry was and is radically challenging in its simplicity. You call us to love others and to be faithful followers of Your truth, even when this goes against the teachings of the day. Give me a heart of obedience so that I might live with the generous wisdom, light, and love of Christ. Amen.

Be Alert

Pray in the Spirit at all times
and on every occasion.
Stay alert and be persistent in your
prayers for all believers everywhere.

EPHESIANS 6:18 NLT

Even in the days of Paul's letter to Corinth, men had to be aware that Satan was prowling the earth to find men weak in their faith. In a very subtle way he would lure them away from the church. Men of the twenty-first century have to be alert that they are targeted for attack.

Become an alert man by being faithful in your prayer life. Be consistent, persistent, and persevering in your prayer so that you remain close in God's care. Ask Him for discernment and wisdom in all that you do.

Many men let their guard down in the area of sexual purity. By allowing their eyes and heart to wander, they struggle with lust. It is important to be alert to your actions and the possible consequences. Stay watchful.

Father God, give me an attentive mind and heart. I want to be on my guard and to seek Your leading in all things. Help me in my areas of weakness. May my heart be alert to Your will. Amen

Stand Firm in the Faith

Take delight in the LORD,
and he will give you the desires of your heart.
Commit your way to the LORD;
trust in him and he will do this:
He will make your righteous
reward shine like the dawn,
your vindication like the noonday sun.

PSALM 37:4-6

Every day, as we get out of bed, we have to commit ourselves to the Lord. By saying a simple prayer and turning our feet and heart toward God, we allow Him to direct our paths. You will experience a vital, rich life when you trust God.

As you stand, walk, talk, and live firmly in your faith, you are better able to avoid the pitfalls that the world presents. We have access to God's power and provision. The righteous life is a bright one. Don't let your thoughts and actions be dimmed by the world's darkness.

Have you surrendered your days to the Lord? Start today. Give Him every area of your life and don't hold anything back from His care. You will lead your family in righteousness and your life will move forward toward God's shining purpose.

God, I give to You my every waking and sleeping moment. I've held back from trusting You with all of my life, but I want to give You all of me. Show me how to trust You more. Amen.

Act Like Men

You, man of God, flee from all this [evil], and
pursue righteousness, godliness, faith, love,
endurance and gentleness.

1 TIMOTHY 6:11

One of the toughest decisions we have to make each day is to become a man of God. In the very beginning, God made us in His image. Men are not to look alike, but we are all to become men of courage and honor. In our verse today, Paul provides Timothy with instruction about how to remain a man of integrity. While the world might say it's okay to dabble in activities that are morally questionable, Paul doesn't hesitate to say to Timothy, "You, man of God, flee from all this!"

We are fortunate to have the convictions of Paul to remind us of where our own convictions should be. Are we being a model of such manhood to our sons, friends, or coworkers? Do our families know without a doubt that we are pursuing righteousness? Be sure the answer is yes. And seek out a mentor who will help you remain accountable to noble behavior.

Father God, You provide us with Your instruction and yet it can be so hard to run from the temptations and the pleasures of the world. I am a new creation. I want to stay true to my manhood as I honor You, my God. Amen.

Be Strong

Be strong and courageous, all you who
put your hope in the LORD!
PSALM 31:24 NLT

The psalmist's call for us to be strong isn't just about physical strength, but is about becoming men who are strong in character. We have to study, commit, and trust God so when we are attacked by evil, we can very confidently say no. Bind evil with righteousness. We must prepare ourselves. If we wait for a tough situation to arise before we are concerned with our strength, it will be too late. Prepare for the days ahead with a solid foundation of scriptural knowledge and spiritual courage. Know what and why you believe as you do. The choices you make today will determine who and where you will be tomorrow. Say no to good things and save your yes for the best.

America truly needs strong and brave men in today's culture. God gave you a role to lead your families. Don't shy away from the call to be strong in the Lord.

Father God, I seek Your Word and Your faithfulness as the sources for my strength. Give me the power of strong character. I want to be prepared so that I don't miss an opportunity to rely on You and to counter evil and ungodliness with Your love and truth. Amen.

A Blessing or a Curse?

Start children off on the way they should go,
and even when they are old they
will not turn from it.

PROVERBS 22:6

When our fourth grandchild, Bradley Joe, graduated from high school, we were so proud of all his accomplishments. He was successful in drama and vocal music activities. He showed leadership skills with his friends. And he remained committed in attending church. This milestone was a wonderful step in the development of his young life.

As we watched him get his diploma, we wondered what the next phase of life would be for him. Was college to be a blessing or curse? Some students struggle when they are away from home. They aren't sure what to do with their new freedoms when they are away from their grounding. They are free to establish new routines without Mom or Dad around.

As we sent off this young man, we prayed that the next four years would be a blessing for him and all of his caring family. Who in your life is facing a new beginning? Pray for them and encourage them to make the new stage a blessing.

Father God, put a protective hedge around our children. Draw them close to Your heart. Clasp Your arms around their bodies and never let go. Amen.

Christian Marriage

By wisdom a house is built, and through
understanding it is established;
through knowledge its rooms are filled
with rare and beautiful treasures.

PROVERBS 24:3-4

One of the great blessings in life is to have a long marriage. Emilie and I have been married more than 57 years. Yet, it seems like yesterday that we stood before our pastor and recited our vows. I'm so blessed to be with a godly woman. I don't lose sight of this truth even when we face obstacles. In fact, both of us feel more blessed to have a marriage built on faith and love when troubles arise. These truths are the foundation of a Christian marriage:

- Christ is at the center of marriages that last.
- Marriage takes work.
- Put your spouse ahead of yourself.

How are you doing in these areas? Do you place God as the center of your relationship? Are you nurturing your marriage in good times and bad? Do you seek out ways to put your wife first? My friend, may you experience the rich reward of a lasting and loving marriage. Today the prayer is for you.

Father God, may the reader today realize that marriage is not easy. Give each of them more patience to hang on to their wedding vows. Amen.

Psalm of Praise I

Praise the LORD, O my soul;
all my inmost being, praise his holy name.

PSALM 103:1

In Psalm 103, we have the example of David's wonderful expressions of thanksgiving to God. Read these wonderful verses to fill your life with praise.

In the early days of our Christian faith these verses were put to music and sung. So to help you memorize God's Word, let's turn back to using music. Think of the "alphabet" song (a, b, c, d…). Try using its tune as you read and memorize the first five verses of Psalm 103:1-5 (adjust the syllables to the tune as needed):

Praise the LORD, my soul, all my inmost being, praise his holy name. Praise the LORD, my soul, and forget not all his benefits—who forgives all your sins and heals all your diseases, who redeems your life from the pit and crowns you with love and compassion, who satisfies your desires with good things so that your youth is renewed like the eagle's.

Recite and sing these verses as you drive, take a shower, work in the yard, and play with your children. Be filled with thanksgiving and you'll notice so much more to be thankful for!

Father God, I want to be a man who thanks You every day for all You have done. May I never forget Your goodness. Amen.

Psalm of Praise II

*[He] satisfies your desires with good things so
that your youth is renewed like the eagle's.*

PSALM 103:5

Let's keep the spirit of praise burning bright. Continue
using the alphabet song or another familiar tune to memorize
Psalm 103:6-11 (adjust the syllables to the tune as needed):

*The LORD works righteousness and justice for all the
oppressed. He made known his ways to Moses, his deeds
to the people of Israel: The LORD is compassionate and
gracious, slow to anger, abounding in love. He will not
always accuse, nor will he harbor his anger forever; he
does not treat us as our sins deserve or repay us according
to our iniquities. For as high as the heavens are above the
earth, so great is his love for those who fear him.*

God's promises are so good to keep close to our hearts.

*Lord, You are my example of strength and tenderness. Give me
a mind that is quick to come up with reasons to praise You and
then let me speak and sing these praises without shame. Amen.*

Psalm of Praise III

*Praise the LORD, all his works everywhere in his
dominion. Praise the LORD, my soul.*

PSALM 103:22

God's grace places our sins far from us. Live your life with
a heart of praise, as David did in Psalm 103:12-22:

*As far as the east is from the west, so far has he removed
our transgressions from us. As a father has compassion on
his children, so the LORD has compassion on those who
fear him; for he knows how we were formed, he remembers that we are dust. The life of mortals is like the grass,
they flourish like a flower of the field…But from everlasting to everlasting the LORD's love is with those who fear
him…The LORD has established his throne in heaven,
and his kingdom rules over all. Praise the LORD…all his
works everywhere in his dominion.*

As David gave us a glimpse at how he expressed his thanks
to the awesome character of God, may we do likewise in
return for who He is.

*Father God, help me to leave the past in the past and embrace
the power of Your grace. When I don't feel worthy of Your love,
remind me that I am Your son. Praise Your holy name. Amen.*

Holy Source of Comfort

Thy rod and thy staff they comfort me.

PSALM 23:4 KJV

When we're in pain, it is logical that we want something that will quickly deaden it. It might be a pill, a drug, a liquid, an injection, an escape, a depression—anything to get us out of our problems. There's a better alternative and that is what the psalmist gives in the famous twenty-third Psalm: "Thy rod and thy staff they comfort me." The shepherd protects his sheep with his rod or club. He uses it to fight off wild beasts and to guide sheep along their way.

Take a look at your life and faith. In what ways do you seek comfort? Where have you sought refuge instead of in God's presence? To live by God's grace is to have God's strength in the day of trouble. Trust it completely and you'll discover the great strength of His care.

Father God, through the years You have protected and guided me with Your rod and staff. You have held me up in times of weakness. I appreciate the strength and comfort You have given me. Amen.

One Minute
Alone with God
Prayer

Father God, You are my shepherd and You know me by name. You notice when I have wandered off on my own, and You search the land for me to bring me back to the flock. I used to think that all I wanted was to be on my own and to not have anyone leading the way. But as time goes by, I understand that the way of life can be rocky and unsure. I find comfort in Your direction and Your pursuit of me. My heart is loyal to You, my shepherd.

Now, when I hear You call my name, I don't hide or run in the other direction. I'm grateful that You care to see me, know me, and show me the way to go. When I hear Your voice, I know that everything will be okay...and I can't wait to be in Your presence and to walk with You. Thank You for changing my heart and for always knowing my name. Amen.

Enemies of Peace

Submit to God and be at peace with him;
in this way prosperity will come to you.

JOB 22:21

There is a great quote from Petrarch: "Five great enemies to peace inhabit with us—avarice, ambition, envy, anger and pride. If those enemies were to be banished, we should infallibly enjoy perpetual peace." These are the same character traits that Jesus taught against. Jesus knew that His teaching would be a sword to the hearers of His day. They are also the sword that divides the warmongers and the peacemakers today. The condition of the heart is what divides the human race. These very same things can derail us from God's will for us unless we change our behaviors, with God's help.

- Avarice (Greed): Instead of fostering greed, nurture your desire to give to others.
- Ambition: Don't let becoming number one override your commitment to the One.
- Envy: You cannot be working on your weaknesses if you are always focused on others.
- Anger: Give your pain and frustrations to the Lord. Ask for peace.
- Pride: When you let your ego go and you embrace humility, you discover true strength.

Which of these areas is a trouble spot?

God, show me how to eliminate these enemies of peace. I want to be compassionate, faithful, persevering, wise, and humble. Give me the courage to become a peacemaker. Amen.

Fix Your Eyes on God

Let your eyes look straight ahead;
fix your gaze directly before you.

PROVERBS 4:25

As a boy, when I went to my PaPa's farm in Texas during the summertime, he would take me along with him to plow his land. He had a team of donkeys and a draft horse to pull the multi-furrow plow. He told me that in order to plow a straight row you have to keep your eyes fixed on a distant object while you're plowing. This principle is also true as we strive to live a straight path in everyday life, if we fix our gaze on Christ.

The complete book of Proverbs is about following a straight path, retaining integrity, avoiding sexual impurity, controlling our speech, getting along with others, and staying healthy.

According to Solomon, the wise person can walk the straight path and not be misdirected.

And when Jesus was talking to Thomas, he said, "I am the way, and the truth, and the life. No one comes to the Father except through me" (John 14:6). So the only way to follow a straight path through life is to keep your eyes on Him.

Father God, let me focus on You, for wisdom begins by having the proper awe for who You are. My purpose in life is to know and enjoy You forever! Amen.

Become an Imitator

*Follow God's example, therefore, as dearly
loved children and walk in the way of love,
just as Christ loved us and gave himself for us
as a fragrant offering and sacrifice to God.*

EPHESIANS 5:1-2

The word *imitation* has a negative connotation in our culture now, but in Ephesians 5, we discover that becoming imitators of God is exactly what we are to strive for. This is a call to be authentic and diligent followers of Christ. We have to *put off* lies, anger, stealing, corrupt speech, bitterness, sexual immorality, foolish talk, and darkness. This passage also lists things we are to *put on*: truth telling, surrender, trust, encouragement, forgiveness, love, thankfulness, and light. You choose.

The world is continually trying to pull us to its ways—but we who are wise will not be led by its cunning ways. Evaluate how you spend your time. Are you a wise or unwise user of your time, both in minutes and in opportunities? Are you spending each day as a window of time to imitate Christ?

Father God, let me pay more attention to how I spent my time. Let me be a wise user of my time. Amen.

When Adversity Strikes

Consider it pure joy, my brothers and sisters,
whenever you face trials of many kinds,
because you know that the testing of your
faith produces perseverance.

JAMES 1:2

We know that Job's trials strengthened his character, and people talk about the patience of Job. But he demonstrated more than patience. He shows us a faith in God that has staying power and is able to endure to the end. Through all of Job's losses and suffering, he did not sin nor did he blame God.

One of my favorite verses in this book is Job's response to his wife's statement: "Are you still maintaining your integrity? Curse God and die!" Our hero responded so beautifully, "Shall we accept good from God, and not trouble?" (Job 2:9-10).

You can rejoice in the Lord in all situations and give thanks for whatever challenges come your way, knowing that God is your faithful Redeemer. When adversity strikes, the strength of the Lord is with you.

God, may I respond as Job did when I am under pressure. Show me what it means to live out Your Word with blamelessness and faithfulness so that I can be a servant who praises You in the midst of trials. Amen.

Celebrating What Remains

I waited patiently for the LORD; he turned to me
and heard my cry. He lifted me out of the slimy
pit, out of the mud and mire; he set my feet upon
a rock and gave me a firm place to stand. He put
a new song in my mouth,
a hymn of praise to God.

PSALM 40:1-3

When Emilie was going through her chemo, radiation, and bone-marrow transplant we saw little hope of us ever having a normal life again. For five long years, our prayers were for that "normal." We looked forward to being able to go to church, have guests in our home, and hug and shake hands with our friends. These ordinary activities became our hope. Now, more than nine years later, we are back doing all those things plus some.

Has an area of your life been turned upside down? Perhaps you've already seen God's restoration and are rejoicing. But you may still be looking out over the vast landscape of loss and uncertain how God is going to bring restoration. Be encouraged and don't give up the fight. You'll be amazed at what God can do.

Father God, give me the courage to fight on when I feel that life has been taken away from me! Let me see light at the end of the tunnel. Amen.

Goodness or Grace?

For we are God's handiwork,
created in Christ Jesus to do good works,
which God prepared in advance for us to do.

EPHESIANS 2:10

Grace is the unearned favor that saves us. It is a free gift from God. In Ephesians, Paul reminds us that before Christ, we were all dead in our sins and trespasses. But through Jesus' sacrifice, He takes us from death to life. His mercy and grace allows for our faith. We don't earn it. Why would God do such a thing? "In order that in the coming ages he might show the incomparable riches of his grace, expressed in his kindness toward us in Christ Jesus" (Ephesians 2:7).

When we accept the gospel, we respond with good works—works cannot save, but good works always accompany salvation. Since we are His workmanship, we become God's poem. We are uniquely designed to perform His work while on earth. We are not here by accident. And when you face discouragement, remember that it is never Your goodness or good acts that save You. It is God's good grace.

Father, I feel empowered by Your will and Your strength to do good. My desire to please You compels me toward service and compassion. At the end of the day, I know that I'm not earning Your grace, but I am reflecting my gratitude for it. Amen.

A Life of Praise

Ascribe to the LORD the glory due his name;
worship the LORD in the splendor of his holiness.

PSALM 29:2

Gaining credit, earning credit, and establishing a solid reputation is what we are geared to do as men in this world. In the workplace, it is very abnormal to not take credit when you've put in the labor and time or the creative energy. But imagine if you gave God the glory and credit for each step you made and for every blessing you experienced? How would your coworkers and friends respond?

When we acknowledge that we make it through the hard times *and* the good times because of God's strength and splendor, those around us receive a bigger picture of God's involvement in our lives. This week, turn any praises you receive upward and give God the glory. Don't do this as a way to draw attention to your faith, but do it with a sincere heart that truly wants to praise its creator and master.

Father God, how often have I taken credit for Your works? Show me what it means to live a life of praise and gratitude. I don't need to earn the world's status in order to give You glory. I praise You because You are holy. Amen.

Yet I Will Rejoice

Though the fig tree does not bud and
there are no grapes on the vines,
though the olive crop fails and the
fields produce no food,
though there are no sheep in the pen
and no cattle in the stalls,
yet I will rejoice in the LORD, I will
be joyful in God my Savior.

HABAKKUK 3:17-18

Believe me when I say that there will be seasons of life when you look around you and life seems barren. Maybe you've gone through or are going through this kind of fruitless season. Do not lose hope. God is not absent.

When Emilie went through painful setbacks in her cancer journey, and when we were both very weary, we didn't lose sight of our source of joy and peace. Our eyes were on Jesus. If this is a trying time, I encourage you to start your morning and end your evening by saying "Yet I will rejoice." You'll notice a shift of perspective and a deepening of faith and assurance. In all that you face, Your Savior is with you. Rejoice.

Jesus, You are my Redeemer, my Savior. Reveal to me the way of all rejoicing. When the harvest of my life seems to be waning, the source of my joy and comfort never is. You are my everlasting love and Lord. Amen.

Believing, Growing, Changing

*It is with your heart that you
believe and are justified,
and it is with your mouth that you
profess your faith and are saved.*

ROMANS 10:10

It hasn't always been easy. I've had to give up much bitterness, anger, fear, hatred, and resentment. Many times, I've
had to back up and start over asking God to take over control
of my life and show me His way to live. But as I have learned
to follow Him, He has guided me through times of pain and
joy, struggle and growth. And how rewarding it has been to
see maturity take root and grow in my life. I give thanks and
praise for His goodness to me over the years.

Growing in godliness is a lifelong process. Invite God into
your heart and life and then be open to the transformation
He'll work in you. It is the best thing you'll ever do because it
is all about God doing things through you.

*Lord, my heart believes in Your salvation and hope. May I
remain open to the changes You require of me. Lead me to praise
You as I believe, grow, and change to become the man You made
me to be. Amen.*

One Minute Alone with God Prayer

Father God, from beginning to end, You are the author of my faith and my life. Give me a desire to grow in Your strength so that I adopt Your character with great conviction and compassion. You are with me in this journey of life. I need never to feel alone or separated from You. When there is distance, I know that I'm giving more weight to worry and to the world's clamor than I am to Your peace and truth.

Draw me to Your presence, God. Show me the way to become a man of goodness and righteousness. I will seek Your voice and Your face every day so that I am able to reflect Your light and love to the people in my life. I want to be the first to praise You in good times and in the middle of hardship. Take my life, God. Shape me into the man of God You want me to become. Amen.

About the Author

For more information about Bob and Emilie Barnes,
their books, and their ministry,
please send a self-addressed, stamped envelope to:

More Hours in My Day
2150 Whitestone Drive
Riverside, CA 92506

Visit:
www.EmilieBarnes.com

Email:
sheri@emiliebarnes.com

Other Books by Bob Barnes

5-Minute Faith Builders for Men

Bob provides insightful, to-the-point devotions to help you discover and apply God's wisdom to your daily life. With down-to-earth style, he encourages you to build a strong relationship with Jesus, use the Bible as your guide, and walk your faith with conviction and gratitude. Rerelease of *Men Under Construction*.

Five Minutes in the Bible for Men

With valuable encouragement from the Bible, bestselling author Bob Barnes provides five-minute thoughts from the Scriptures to give you strength on your way. It shows you how to help you and other men grow in grace by how you build each other up with your words and hold one another to a high standard, turning to God's Word to guide you daily.

You aren't built to be without relationships with other men. Most importantly, real men really need God.

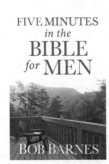

Other Great Books for Men

One-Minute Prayers™ for Men
by Hope Lyda

As you fulfill your commitments, care for your family, and seek your life's purpose, you face a multitude of demands and expectations. In the presence of God you will find respite and strength. These themed, brief prayers draw you to the feet of Jesus where wisdom, direction, and guidance are offered.

A Look at Life from the Deer Stand Devotional
by Steve Chapman

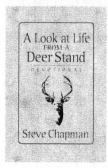

Steve Chapman, avid hunter and best-selling author of *A Look at Life from a Deer Stand* (more than 300,000 copies sold), has a gift for gleaning faith lessons from the glories of creation. Each devotion begins with the inspiration of a Scripture verse and closes with the stillness of a prayer. You will be excited by the application of biblical wisdom, delighted by the humor, caught up in the adventure of hunting, and intrigued by the exploration of God's character.